it's REALLY 10 months™

SPECIAL DELIVERY

A collection of stories from girth to birth

COMPILED BY:

NATALIE GUENTHER, KIM SCHENKELBERG, CELESTE SNODGRASS

Omaha, Nebraska

Contact: ItsReally10Months@gmail.com
www.ItsReally10Months.com

Paperback ISBN: 978-0-9888668-4-3
Mobi ISBN: 978-0-9888668-5-0
EPUB ISBN: 978-0-9888668-6-7

LCCN: 2015947880
Library of Congress Cataloging information on file with publisher.

Design and production: Concierge Marketing, Inc.
Printed in the United States of America.

10 9 8 7 6 5

To our families. Thank you for putting up with our faces being in our phones too much, our late night meetings and our terrible inside jokes. We love you all and are so thankful you love us unconditionally. Without you, none of this would be possible. We promise not to do another book. Until the next one.

Acknowledgments

We'd like to give a shout out to a few amazing ladies that helped us out along the way. First of all, we were honored to work with the smart, talented and wickedly funny Nicole Leigh Shaw. We met her a little over a year ago, fan-girled all over her and somehow twisted her arm into being our editor. This work shines but she made it shine brighter. Thank you dear lady.

Amy Morrison from Pregnant Chicken. This woman, this saint, this beacon of light took us right under her chicken wing. She cheered for us, she shared our stuff, she was just nice. It can't just be because she's Canadian—we think she's actually a genuinely nice person. We promise to buy her as many Snapples and American candies as her little chicken wings can carry.

To our contributors. Thank you all for trusting us with your words and your talent. You are such a gifted bunch of writers. We are so thrilled to be able to collect your words and share them with the world. You worked hard. We owe you a frosty adult beverage and a hug.

Celeste, Kim & Natalie

Contents

Introduction 1

The Pluses and Minuses of Pregnancy. 3
—Susanne Kerns

Baked Potatoes are an Instrument of the Devil 9
—Carrie Groves

Bringing Home Baby 13
—Alessandra Macaluso

The Great Bowel Escape 21
—Holly Rust

Breech, I Will Turn You. 27
—Julia Goddard

Storm Before the Calm 35
—Lynn Adams

Bless the Baby, but Fuck all of the Fluids 41
—Kathryn Leehane

Four is the Magic Number 47
—Ashli Brehm

Life's Disgusting Miracle: A Father's
Thoughts on Witnessing Labor and Delivery.....................53
    —Richard Black

The Elephant Man in My Vagina 61
    —Teri Biebel

Like Father, Like Sons 65
    —Bethany Meyer

Ten Signs You are Entering the Three-Under-Three Club 73
    —Lea Grover

Hold Up Your Hold Up, She Needs a Burrito....................77
    —Chris Smyrl

I Never Planned on Being a Parent 81
    —Sarah Bregel

Feet in the Air...85
    —Emily Ballard

How Leap Year Ruined My Birth Plan 91
    —Meredith Napolitano

Water, Water Everywhere and Not a Drop to Drink..............99
    —Christina Antus

The Piercing Incident.....................................103
    —Amy Hunter

Labor, Delivery, and Naked Driving 109
    —Mary Widdicks

That's Not Sweat 115
    —Jessica Azar

Beware the Advice Brigade! 121
    —Melissa Charles

.

This Ain't Your Mama's Birth 127
        —Lisa René LeClair

Do Not Touch a Pregnant Woman's Belly Without Asking 133
        —Sarah Cottrell

Sometimes They Birth Themselves 139
        —Sharon Buckley

My Pregnant Nose 145
        —Kate Parlin

The Eviction Notice, Back Labor and Retribution. 151
        —Chris Dean

Pregnantpause. 157
        —Lucia Paul

The Queen of Thrones 161
        —Cate Pedersen

Are You Shitting Me? The Things
They Never Tell You About Childbirth 167
        —Megan Woolsey

Humpty Dumpty, Dissolvable Stitches,
and 'No Chance Underpants' 173
        —Alice Gomstyn

10 Ways to Know You Aren't Done Having Kids. 177
        —Amanda Mushro

Good Advice. 183
        —Megan Steusloff

Author Social Media Appendix 189

The Brains Behind This Book. 195

Introduction

Our first book, *It's Really 10 Months: Delivering the truth about the glow of pregnancy and other blatant lies,* was written by accident. Those private emails were never supposed to be public, but thanks to Celeste and her knack for never deleting anything, our book was born. Throughout the process we grew past being friends and became family. The common thread of pregnancy, labor and delivery tied us close but publishing a book together sealed the deal. After our book was published, we heard from hundreds of women. They said things like: "you guys get it," "that happened to me" and our favorite, "you guys told me everything I needed to know." Connecting with other women catapulted us to our mission today. We do not want women to feel alone during their pregnancy; we want women to feel like they have a safe place to come to celebrate, cry, whine, and worry! We had each other as a supportive tribe of friends and now we deliver that feeling of belonging to a tribe to you through these stories.

The Pluses and
Minuses of Pregnancy

 Susanne Kerns

Like most women, I spent much of early adulthood trying not to get pregnant. I spent a fortune on birth control and weeks of my life panicking after forgetting to take a pill at the right time (or at all). After years of this conditioning, I grew to expect that any unprotected sexual encounter would immediately result in pregnancy.

That is, until we started trying to get pregnant.

When you're trying to get pregnant, there are charts and basal thermometers and mucous calendars and about a dozen other things that make you wonder, "Why did I ever even bother using birth control if it's this hard to get pregnant?"

Fortunately, my first pregnancy was straight out of a '50s television series. We decided it would be perfect if we had a baby in early summer to coincide with my husband's MBA summer break, so we counted back forty weeks on the calendar and got to work. I became pregnant after the first try and spent the remainder of my pregnancy bouncing around all perky and energetic, doing prenatal yoga, and even taking a trip to Sweden at five months to pick up our new cliché Volvo.

Right on cue, at week thirty-nine, my water broke, we went to the hospital, I got my beloved epidural and a few hours later the nurse walked into our birthing suite and said, "Would you mind pausing your movie, your baby is about to fall out." Three minutes and a couple of pushes later, we met our perfect baby girl. Wow, this pregnancy thing is a piece of cake!

Fast-forward four years.

After much deliberation, we were finally ready to try for baby number two. Based on our first child, that just meant we needed to pick a desired due date and back out forty weeks, right? Easy peasy.

Until we had a negative pregnancy test.

And then another negative test.

And then a couple positive tests that became negative tests.

That joke about how "you can't be a little pregnant" ceases to be funny after you actually have a nurse call you with your blood-test results and tell you "you were a little pregnant, but now you're not anymore."

And that's how I learned the term "chemical pregnancy."

A chemical pregnancy is when things start off well enough to release the chemicals that tell your body that you're pregnant, but something happens along the way to make the pregnancy unsustainable.

Chemical pregnancies come and go so quickly that most women never even know if they've had one. However, if you're like me and start taking bulk-packs worth of early-results tests the second the box says you can, a chemical pregnancy will show up early on as a plus sign. Naturally, my heart immediately swelled with false hopes as my head filled with dreams about our little plus sign. Until a few days later, when my hopes began to fade as my continued obsessive test taking now resulted in a (literally) fading plus sign that then became a minus the next day.

I only told a couple close friends about my situation. It's a hard thing to talk about, especially with dear friends who have experienced the heartbreak of miscarriages or who are in the middle of fertility treatments. It felt insensitive to even try to compare my situation to theirs. But sadly, a heart still grieves even after only a few days of dreaming about a little plus sign.

After a couple of these chemical pregnancies, I stopped trusting the tests. After the third, I stopped trusting my body. It was then that I started demanding answers. I was told by doctors that I really shouldn't start worrying until trying unsuccessfully for a year. But at age thirty-seven, I didn't feel like I had the luxury of time and insisted on moving forward with some blood tests.

And it was a good thing I did, because a dozen blood panels later, my doctor told me that I had a blood clotting condition that was causing the chemical pregnancies. My gynecologist recommended starting aspirin therapy in order to try to get pregnant, and told me I would likely need to continue taking it through the entire pregnancy. (You know, aspirin. The stuff that all the pregnancy books say to take only if you've run out of cocaine and heroin.)

To my surprise, the next month I was pregnant. I not only passed my collection of home pregnancy tests, but also passed all the blood tests at the doctor's office. It was official, at the ripe old age of thirty-seven, I was now a "geriatric" pregnant woman. (I'm not saying this to be dramatic; that is the actual medical term for a pregnant woman over the age of thirty-five.) Now, I've had plenty of friends over the age of thirty-five who had normal, problem-free pregnancies. But over the next forty weeks, I managed to make "geriatric" sound like a compliment.

There were the potentially serious issues, like discovering a placental abruption (don't Google that) at week eight, which resulted in an emergency return from a vacation in Whistler as well as weekly ultrasounds throughout my first trimester.

There were the "in my head" issues, like when I celebrated my final your abruption is stable ultrasound with a Subway sandwich, only to remember after the last bite that you're not supposed to eat lunch meat while pregnant. Damn you, listeriosis! (Don't Google that either.)

Then there was the first trimester screening test. Since I was no stranger to ultrasounds, I thought that this was going to be a cake walk, but that's when they discovered an issue with the tubes connecting the baby's kidneys and bladder: vesicoureteral reflux (definitely don't Google that.)

Back to the weekly office visits. This kid was becoming the Kim Kardashian of ultrasounds.

Just so the baby wasn't getting all the attention, I decided to develop some issues of my own, like world-record hemorrhoids and an ectopic heartbeat. (You can Google ectopic heartbeat because it's common and harmless, but never, ever Google hemorrhoids. You can't unsee these things.)

The two of us were quite a pair.

I should have been a nervous wreck but I kept coming back to the words of my wise (or perhaps just crazy), old-school pediatrician told me when I went to him to ask about the baby's kidney issues.

He said, "We know too much these days. All those ultrasounds are like reading tea leaves. If this was twenty years ago, you would have never heard the term 'vesicoureteral reflux.' Mark my words, within a couple years, your baby's kidney issues will completely resolve on their own and you never should have had to have known or worried about them." (I'm sure that he would agree that you should really never Google any medical condition.)

Now, I think he was a bit extreme dismissing tests that diagnose issues that benefit from early detection, but in this particular case he ended up being right. And even if he was just making it up to make me feel better, his assurance gave me the perspective I needed to keep from being a nervous wreck for the next six months.

Six more months! How was it that it was only the fourth month of pregnancy and we have encountered all of these issues? At this stage in my first pregnancy my only concern was planning our trip to Sweden to pick up a car. Last time I was bounding around energetically, but now I found myself moving carefully, convinced that my body hadn't run out of ways to jeopardize this baby. I wouldn't even lift my daughter anymore, instead she and I concocted an elaborate series of steps to get her into shopping carts from a standing position in the back of our mini-van.

Fortunately, the one thing this pregnancy did have in common with my first (aside from compression stockings and hemorrhoids) was a comically fast delivery. Five pushes and five minutes after it started, we were face to face with our perfect baby boy. Both the nurse and doctor were so amazed that they said, "Wow, your body is made for having babies!"

I decided not to point out all the ways my body had proven them wrong in the past two years. Instead I focused on being grateful that my body, which had not been very welcoming to my baby, at least granted him a final kindness of giving him an uncomplicated exit.

That little baby is five years old now. As the pediatrician predicted, his kidney issues did resolve on their own. Aside from his fondness for trying to wrestle himself and telling nonsensical knock-knock jokes, there don't appear to be any long-term effects from the aspirin, dozens of ultrasounds, or the Subway sandwich.

When I think back to that pregnancy, three things are clear: First, it's a good thing that it wasn't my first pregnancy or else I don't think there would have been a second. Next, despite my body being "made for having babies," this would officially be our last. But most importantly, even considering everything that we went through, I wouldn't change a thing because, in the end, it means having the gift of this sweet, silly, funny, perfect boy in our lives.

Susanne Kerns

Once upon a time, Susanne Kerns was a senior account director at an advertising agency working for two of the top brands in the world. Nine years ago she traded in her corporate life for a life as a stay at home mom, raising two of the best kids in the world. She started her blog, TheDustyParachute.com, as a way to dust off her online advertising skills and begin her job search. Instead, she now uses it as a way to spend lots of time on the computer so her kids think that mommy has a job.

Baked Potatoes are an Instrument of the Devil

 Carrie Groves

Hormones. They are enough to make you shank a bitch when you're not pregnant, but when you have an explosion of cells in your uterus dividing to generate a new human being, they will give you more personalities than Sybil, and there are times when they may all come out at once.

I would like to say that I was the exception, and that I never rode even one emotional roller coaster for those many months, but I would be lying.

The weight of my emotions was at times too much to bear, like when my dog had explosive diarrhea all throughout the house and I was the only one at home to clean it up, or when I tried on maternity pants and was devastated because I wasn't big enough for them yet. Too fat for regular pants, but not pregnant enough for maternity wear. It was a cruel time.

But what brought me to my lowest low during pregnancy was the most mundane of items: a baked potato.

When I got pregnant, my friends were green with envy. Not because I was growing a beautiful little life, but because they thought I was going to be able to eat whatever I wanted for the next nine months.

We were women creeping up on thirty, and our metabolisms were not what they were in college. Our excesses were evident on our hips, and we would have given our love handles to be able to indulge in chocolate lava cake or apple martinis once again.

If only they knew that it was all a horrible lie. For the first trimester you're in a constant state of hangover with a side of PMS-on-steroids. Who wants to eat an endless buffet of deliciousness when it will inevitably come right back up and into your toilet? Let me tell you, those spicy tacos will rip you a new esophagus the second time around, and your broken boobs will not thank you when you slam them up against the bowl as you retch.

The last trimester is not much better because the lovely little being you're growing is pushing all of your insides out and karate chopping your kidneys as they complete the hostile takeover of your uterus. During this time, the sad fact is, there is no room for food.

Now, smack dab in the middle of those two hellish trimesters is the sweet spot of pregnancy. You're over the nausea, the hips have stopped their glacial spread, and you don't look like a parade float, yet. It's beautiful, really. This is when the cravings happen.

You hear the stories about women waking up at 2 am and pushing their partner out of bed to get them ice cream, grilled cheese, or whatever it is "the baby" wants. That's really more of a myth. The truth is, women become more susceptible to suggestion.

When I'm not pregnant, I hate fast food. I've watched too many of those hidden camera shows and I am firm in my belief that my taco shell has been licked or my mayo has semen in it. But once I was knocked up, it was a completely different story. If I saw an Arby's commercial for fish sandwiches, I had to have one. With a milkshake. And it couldn't be anywhere else but Arby's. There would be consequences if someone tried to trick me with a McDonald's fish sandwich.

Of course, my husband was overjoyed because it meant that he finally got to eat at all of those places that I refused to go. He probably hoped that I would stay pregnant forever.

One day, I was at work and I had a craving for a baked potato and salad from Wendy's. I could picture the potato, the sour cream, and the butter working its way down to my belly. I had to have it.

I moseyed my way to the nearest Wendy's and got ready for what was going to be the best baked potato of my life. I mean, if I wanted it so much, it was going to taste fantastic, right?

Wrong.

When I got to the head of the line and placed my order, I heard the words no pregnant woman wants to hear. "I'm sorry ma'am, but we're out of baked potatoes."

What!? Out of baked potatoes? What totalitarian regime do I live under where a pregnant woman can't get a baked potato? Do I need to move to Canada to get a decent lunch and socialized prenatal care?

My world spun and I was at a loss. Sure, I could have ordered the salad I planned on and a Frosty, but it wasn't the same. I wanted my potato, dammit. Nothing else would do.

Holding my head high, I left. I walked slowly out to my car, trying to process what just happened. It was incomprehensible. Here I am trying to grow another human being, and all I ask for in return is a baked potato. It was not too much to ask.

The great sadness over the potato loss overwhelmed me and I burst into tears. I cried for a good five minutes over my lost spud, mourning its soft, hot deliciousness.

Yes, I cried over a baked potato. Now, if that was not my hormones completely dicking me over, I don't know what is.

Don't get me wrong, these hormones also made me crave glorious milkshakes that I enjoyed on a regular basis, tomato sauce by the spoonful, and I swear they made orange juice taste as sweet as if I sucked it from the original orange itself.

There were times when the food was better than sex. True story.

Looking back, the hormones were like a bad boyfriend. He would speak sweetly to me, whispering how happy he was, and then he would whip around and slap me in the face with a potato.

Oh, I am so glad we broke up. To quote Taylor Swift, "We are never, ever, ever, getting back together." I don't care how tasty your potatoes are.

Carrie Groves

Carrie Groves is the author of the blog PoniesAndMartinis.com. When she is not trying to keep her kids and dogs in line, she enjoys wine, writing, and song. Carrie is a regular contributor to *BLUNTmoms*, and has been featured on *Mamapedia* and *Mamalode*.

Bringing Home Baby

Alessandra Macaluso

Toward the end of my pregnancy I thought a lot about how I felt: tired from uncomfortable sleepless nights, a bit anxious, and very much like a wild animal. I also worried a lot about labor and delivery. It's only natural—delivering your baby is the most mind-blowing, incredible moment of your life! I also thought, at least a tiny bit, about what would happen once we got our baby home, like where she would sleep, what items we'd use from our registry, and whether or not I'd return to work.

What I did not think much about was the space between when we'd prepare to exit the hospital and getting settled in with our little one. It was in this space where I learned things no one could prepare me for or forewarn me about in my birth classes.

Let's consider the sick joke that is the reality of a woman bringing home a new baby. You're recovering from either a vaginal birth or a C-section, you're hopped up on pain meds, and your hormones are playing ping-pong. Your nipples might be bleeding from breastfeeding. You're exhausted. And oh, here's a completely dependent human baby to care for. Catch! There's a reason why these experiences are given to women only. Men would lose their shit!

Considering all of the above, things may not go as planned while you adjust to your new role, and that's okay. I'm here to share with you a list of my own failures, surprises, and disappointments between the time my baby was delivered and those first few nights at home.

Let's start with the most uncomfortable of them, shall we?

The catheter. I had never had a catheter before, but because I needed a C-section, I had the joy of experiencing one. I was told it would be removed around midnight that first night and I couldn't wait because I was already so tired of being "hooked up" to things. So the clock struck twelve and in rode my nurse in catheter-removing armor.

As she prepared for removal, I asked, "Will this hurt?"

"Maybe. It does for some people," she said. My anxiety began to ascend. But before I reached full altitude, she declared, "All done!" I couldn't believe it. No pain! I was free of the pee tube!

But, suddenly, it was as if my sweet nurse morphed into the scary guy from those *Saw* movies, when out of her mouth came, "You have four hours to urinate on your own. If you don't in time, we'll have to put another one in." She left.

I stared at the clock. I can do this, right? I've been peeing for thirty-two years! I scooted out of bed, made my way to the toilet, and nothing. This lasted for three and a half hours. I dragged myself out of the bed in hopes of a tinkle, only to come up with unusable toots and some blood. Nurse *Saw* came back at 3:45 am. "Anything?"

I shook my head, defeated. She produced a catheter out of her pocket. "I'll just set this down right here, and I'll be back in fifteen minutes."

I'm happy to report that the sight of that second catheter literally scared the piss out of me.

Confusion about breastfeeding. While at the hospital, ask a lactation consultant for advice. I dare you. While you'll get some valuable information, each has their own techniques and rules, and they often contradict one another. One will say to make a "sandwich" with your boob, another will tell you to switch boobs mid-feeding, and a third will say that the trick is to stick one thumb up your ass, jump up and down, and jiggle your left boob for the Magic Milk to start flowing.

You might also have the urge to punch at least one consultant in the face. I'll never forget when I asked one, through clenched teeth and teary eyes, as my baby piranha nursed, "Is it supposed to hurt?" and she responded, "No. Breastfeeding shouldn't hurt." Really, lady? I don't know what you do with your nipples on the weekends that would make something like this not hurt, but I imagine it involves jumper cables and a copy of *Fifty Shades of Grey*.

The "coming home" outfit. You might have already chosen one for your baby. We had such an adorable one for Penelope! My brother and his fiancée gave it to us. It was blue with white polka dots, featuring a little red crab on it—perfect for July.

But it didn't matter, because we never put it on her. We put nothing on her, as in "naked baby exits hospital in hospital-provided diaper and poor attempt at a swaddle" nothing.

How did this happen? I know some love their hospital stay, but after two nights of interruption and discomfort, I didn't belong to that camp. I wanted my own bed and shower, was tired of being poked at, and couldn't wait to bring Penelope home.

When the docs said we could leave a day early we Did. Not. Mess. Around. We were also told that we had thirty minutes to pack up and get—um, I mean check—out. In the blur that was the first two days after becoming parents, we hadn't yet had to dress our baby, so that polka-dot crab outfit with all those snaps and holes for tiny newborn extremities looked as easy to put on her as disassembling a bomb. So, diaper and swaddle it was. My advice is, select a coming home outfit that doesn't go over your baby's head (because crap, that's scary for a first-time mom), and ask a nurse for help.

The hospital exit. We had to stop at the nurse's station so they could remove Penelope's ankle security bracelet (which made me feel better, because I had only been a mom for forty-eight hours and was already starting to feel like Dina Lohan). Then we made our way toward the elevator to head downstairs, and when the doors opened, so did the floodgates to Penelope's vocal chords; out of nowhere my sweet, peaceful baby went full-out ape shit.

The elevator filled with people, including another new mom who appeared totally put together. Her new baby was decked out in jewels and glitter and pink bling-y blankets, leading me to one conclusion: that her aunt was one of the Real Housewives of New Jersey. The baby smelled like Chanel No. 5.

I grabbed the corner of the hospital swaddle and pulled it tighter around Penelope. As she continued to scream her head off, a nurse yelled, in a thick Jamaican accent: "Sing to her! She'll stop crying." All I could think was, *If I sing to her, she'll cry harder.* Then I started crying, because I had no idea what I was doing with my new baby, had no business being a mom, and I am no Norah Jones. To recap, Penelope's crying, I'm crying, I'm already being told what to do, and no one is singing "Come Away with Me."

Your baby might scream and cry, and you might feel like it's all your fault. It's not. Babies cry. They eventually stop.

The "mom cradle" fail. I exited the elevator to wait in that area where the new moms sit patiently in their wheelchairs, cradling their bundles of joy.

Although my little girl was only two days old, we'd already figured out the only thing that seemed to calm her was when we held her out in front of us, straight up and down, bouncing her slightly. (Maybe because she was breech, this soothed her?) So there I was, amongst the cradling, cooing mothers, holding my wailing, naked baby out in front of me as if she were a tiny little puppy with mud on her paws. "This helps her stop crying," I stammered to a nearby mom who side-eyed me as she held her child like a normal baby. She undoubtedly mentally awarded me "Mom of the Year," and I hadn't even exited the hospital yet.

But guess what? Penelope stopped crying. It was my first of many moments where I ignored the fact that I looked like a total moron and did what I knew was best for my baby.

Once home, I made some ridiculous statements. New mom fog? Check. No sleep? Check. Delirious, in pain, in shock? Check, check, check. So I did what could only be expected of someone in my state. I confused our daughter's behavior with that of our cats. Here is an actual conversation I had with my husband.

"What's wrong?" my husband asked.

"I don't think (*sniffle sniffle*) she likes me."

"What!? She's sleeping on you! She's so content right now!"

"Well then why (*sniffle*) isn't she purring!?"

I wish I were making that up. It's funny now, but the disappointment I felt when my daughter did not purr was real. New motherhood will do that to you. Expect it. Don't be alarmed. Try to laugh at yourself. Then do like Elsa and "Let it goooo."

You may experience terror like never before. It was the second night home with Penelope and it seemed like nothing we did could console her. I had nursed her for what felt like the millionth time and my nipples were on fire. A wave of terror washed over me. I grabbed a fistful of hair with each hand and yelled, "What did we do!? What did we *do*?"

Clearly someone made a mistake! Surely we weren't cut out for this. Our lives would never be the same! Oh, I was a terrible mother, I knew it!

Only, I wasn't. I was simply experiencing the shock that occurs once the nurses are gone, the frozen lasagnas are eaten, and it's just you, your baby, and your husband. It was a scary, mind-altering moment when it became real that there was no going back, and I've never been more afraid in my life. But I'm here to tell you, it passed. If you feel overwhelmed, let it happen, and know that it will pass—I promise.

What I learned is that you can prepare all you want, but nothing can set you up for when you take that baby, your baby, home for the first time. I read the books. My baby whispered to me. And do you know what she said? "Pssst. You don't know what you're doing."

Fast forward eighteen months and I've realized it doesn't matter. Because I now know the dirty little secret of parenthood: None of us really know what we're doing. We're all improvising. We're making mistakes, making things up, and surprising ourselves in both how much we know and how much we don't. Keeping it all together while keeping our fingers crossed that nothing falls apart. Letting go of ideas of perfection and plans, because the former doesn't exist, and any attempts at the latter are comical at best.

So give some thought to the space between giving birth and settling in with your baby. Allow yourself a whole lot of room for adjustment, and a big fat permission slip to feel all sorts of crazy. While some say "motherhood comes naturally" for many of us, there is a grace period, and that's putting it gently. Things won't go as planned and that's okay.

As for me, I will not beat myself up over things I didn't get "right" the first time, and expect that there will be more where that came from. Number two is growing in my belly as I type. This time around, I might dress her before leaving the hospital. And I'll probably calm the hell down when she doesn't purr.

Alessandra Macaluso

Alessandra Macaluso is an author, freelance writer, and blogger. She is a regular contributor for *The Huffington Post* and *Scary Mommy*, and runs the blog PunkWife.com. Her work has been featured in many other publications and anthologies, which can all be found on her blogs, along with her current projects. She also writes screenplays, and her original screenplay *Polar Suburbia* placed as a semi-finalist in the 2009 Moondance Film Festival. She lives in Charlotte, NC, with her husband, daughter, soon-to-arrive little boy, and a twenty-five-pound cat named Marcus who believes he is a dog.

The Great Bowel Escape

 Holly Rust

When you're pregnant with your first child, most hospitals offer a class to prepare you for what's to come. It's typically a full day event and the class is packed with new parents, all of which look like deer in headlights. I registered for the class because I wanted to hear all the details firsthand from a medical professional, versus relying on Google. Up to this point, Google had only escalated my anxiety.

Throughout the eight-hour course they reviewed breathing and massaging techniques, discussed pain options, went through the process of dilation, touched briefly on aftercare, and finished off by showing already terrified mothers a video of a baby barbarically pushing itself through a woman's pelvic bone. Suddenly we all felt a little more nauseous.

When the class was over, I left disappointed and even more scared. I felt like I had so many questions, but didn't know exactly how to ask them without sounding like a deranged lunatic. I needed some clarity on things. I wanted to know the nitty-gritty of giving birth—you know, the stuff people conveniently forget to tell you. The stuff that nurses go back to the stations and gossip about. The stuff that doctors divulge at a holiday party after a few cocktails. I didn't want to be that story, or if I was going to be, I at least wanted to be prepared. The moderators either choose to leave this stuff out, or people in the class were just too afraid to ask. I'm sure it was a little bit of both. I couldn't have been the only one in the room wanting to know more about the embarrassing stuff, right?

Personally, my biggest fear of childbirth was (cough) losing my bowels. If any woman says this isn't a fear, she's lying. I'll take it for the team and say we're all worried about that. I wanted to keep some shred of dignity in the delivery room, as I already had to lie there with my legs spread and let every doctor, resident, and nurse get to third base. I also didn't want my son growing up hearing how he came into this world covered in poo.

I know, shouldn't I be worried about more important things like contractions, complications, the epidural not working, or the baby getting stuck? You're right, I was worried about all of that, too, but I had faith the doctors could handle those situations and keep my baby and me safe. It was the embarrassment, the stigma, and the thought of going to the bathroom in front of my husband and a ton of strangers that haunted my dreams at night.

I wanted to know the protocol. I wanted to know the contingency plan. How often does it happen? What are the statistics? Is it really that big of a deal? Do the nurses out you in front of everyone, or pull a Houdini and make it quickly disappear as to not blow your cover? Will they clean your baby up before they hand him/her to you? Do you have to lay in it until the baby comes out? Will everyone be grossed out? Will my husband secretly want a divorce after being utterly disgusted? Will he ever find me sexy again? I needed answers.

Not satisfied with what I learned in class, I turned to my friends. I sent an email to any friend I could think of that was a mom and had a reputation of over sharing.

"Listen ladies, as a control freak and someone who may suffer from a slight case of OCD, I need to know: did you, you know, poop while in labor? Do you know anyone who has? Am I blowing this out of proportion? Spare me the niceties and just give it to me straight. Details, in this case, are appreciated. I need to prepare myself in case—gasp—it happens to me. Thanks in advance."

The few that did respond collectively said that at the end of the day, when the pain kicked in, I wasn't going to give a shit. No pun intended. Then they followed up with saying I should probably see a therapist. Maybe they were right.

A few weeks later when my water broke, I was still living in my anxiety-poop bubble. The whole cab ride over to the hospital I prayed to God. In my prayers I included all of the obligatory stuff like easy delivery, keep me safe, give us a healthy baby, blah blah blah, then concluded with a special request: Please keep my poop inside me and off my baby. Father, Son, Holy Ghost. Amen.

Once I settled into my labor and delivery room, I decided to have a come-to-Jesus chat with my husband.

"Honey, you know I'm terrified. I hate not knowing what to expect. The anticipation is making it worse. As you know, throughout this pregnancy I've had to throw all humility out the window, which isn't easy for me. I know you love me and don't care about stuff like that, but there are a few things I need to just keep between the doctors and my vagina.

"So, with that said, I need you to swear on our love that you will keep your eyes planted firmly above my belly. It's important to me to preserve whatever sexy I have left. No exceptions. I know you'll thank me later. Deal?"

He agreed without any negotiating, which was out of character for him. I secretly think he was relieved. After our conversation I started to feel a little more relaxed, but still anxious.

Over the next few hours, I was sure to be the perfect patient. Nurses are the last people you want on your bad side, especially during labor. I also wanted these ladies to come to my rescue should the unthinkable happen.

When my husband left to get a quick bite to eat, I started sparking up conversation with my nurse. Once I felt like I entered the trust circle, I started asking her more personal questions. Does she have kids? Is it true being a mom is the most amazing thing ever? Is she having any more? Did she have an epidural? What were her recommendations? Then—you guessed it—I dropped the bomb, figuratively. "Do women usually, um, like, go to the bathroom on their babies?"

I expected a graceful, well-versed answer to calm my nerves seeing as she went through this on a daily basis. Her reply was a very nonchalant, "Yes." Then silence.

From there she must have seen the look of sheer terror in my eyes, so she followed up by telling me it was no big deal and they have seen worse. Wait? Worse? Great.

Once my husband arrived back in the room, my contractions started getting unbearable. I tried to work through them with breathing, rotating my hips on a ball, getting on my hands and knees, but nothing was easing the pain. I then realized my friends were right. The local news channel could've come in the room and filmed me wailing like a wild boar and showcased my enormous backside and I wouldn't have thought twice. The only thing on my mind now was drugs—good ones.

Once I got the epidural, I tried to rest. I needed to—after all, I'd been in labor for eleven hours. I checked Facebook, updated my family, and let my girlfriends know that my bowels hadn't emptied, so far.

A few more hours passed and it was time to push so I reminded my husband of his promise. Thankfully, he told me he remembered he was to avert his eyes, right before a nurse asked if I wanted to hold a mirror to watch the birth. We both shook our heads vigorously from side to side, the international sign for "hell no!"

The nurse I'd let into my circle of trust had instructed my husband to scoot my IV monitor back along with all my wires, so he could stand next to me and help hold my legs. As he was following her instructions, she pulled me up to a sitting position, and then quickly laid me back down. Her wide-eyed glare spiked my heart rate. Now what? Was my baby's head out? I couldn't feel anything from the waist down. Then I saw her cat-like reflexes bundle up the little hospital pad I was laying on and run it over to the large trash bin by the door. She came back, grabbed my hand and winked at me just as my husband had finished his task and the doctor entered the room.

Wait, did I—? Did she—? Yes, she did. She was a magician! She saved my dignity! I didn't feel anything. I had no idea my body betrayed me, but most importantly, neither did anyone else!

Suddenly, I was excited. Excited my nightmare was over. Excited the scenario built up in my head turned out to be anticlimactic. Now, I could turn my attention to meeting this little human I'd been growing in my belly for what seemed like decades. My emotions took over and the tears flowed. My birth experience was turning out to be like the one I had always hoped for. After a few short pushes, my son was here. He was beautiful. He was angelic. He was perfect. Ten fingers. Ten toes. Poop free.

Holly Rust

Holly is a native Texan but is currently living in the great city of Chicago with her husband, two sons, and a Chihuahua. Aside from chasing around two lunatic toddlers all day, she is a professional writer. You can read about how she handles her toddler shenanigans on her humor blog, MothersGuidetoSanity.com, which was featured on *The TODAY Show*'s List of Funniest Parents on Facebook. She is a contributor for *The Huffington Post*, *Scary Mommy*, *Dot Complicated*, and The TODAY Parenting Team. You can also find her essays published in several anthologies.

Breech, I Will Turn You

 Julia Goddard

"Oh, no! He's breech!" the ultrasound technician exclaimed a little too loudly for this 32-week pregnant, first-time mom.

"What does that mean?" I was nervous. Up until this moment, my pregnancy had been rather uneventful.

"The doctor will speak to you about your options," she said, handing me a paper towel to wipe off the cold blue goo from my exposed and protruding belly.

Oh no, indeed. This can't be good, I thought.

While waiting for the doctor to come in, I Google searched "32 weeks breech" on my iPhone. Waiting for the results to load, I started to panic. My vision of my beautifully natural, un-medicated vaginal delivery was beginning to slip away. My doctor came in and closed the door. She is always a very calm and authentically cheery person. Just seeing her put me at ease. I put my phone down.

"Hi, Julia. I hear our little friend is breech. Well, it's still early enough that he will likely turn on his own. There are some exercises you might want to try. There isn't really any evidence that they work, but they can't hurt to try if you want to. We will just continue to monitor him and go from there."

All I heard was "you can turn him yourself." My plan was still on track.

I went home determined to be the master of my own labor and delivery. I read everything I could about turning a breech baby so I could have the delivery I wanted.

First, I tried reasoning with him. "Little baby, I have written a detailed plan of your birth including dimly lit candles, Enya playing in the background, wearing my own nightgown, and then you quietly entering this world by passing through my vagina. So, you just need to turn around so that can happen. Okay? Thanks."

I rubbed his head—the hard, orange-sized bump on the top of my belly close to my ribs. No change. Still breech.

Time for phase two. I called my husband, Brian, and asked him to pick up a bag of frozen peas on his way home. Different than my usual pint of Ben and Jerry's Chubby Hubby order, but my husband had already learned not to question my growing number of bizarre requests. "Sure thing, honey. See you at home. Love you."

Brian walked through the front door to find me lying upside-down on top of an ironing board that was leaning against the couch. I was shining a light in between my legs chanting, "Go toward the light, little one. Go towards the light."

He approached with caution, and in his sweetest voice asked about my day.

"How was your doctor's appointment?"

"Good, baby is healthy. My blood pressure levels are normal, but your son is a little directionally challenged at the moment. But don't worry, I have a plan."

He handed me the frozen bag of peas. I placed them on top of my belly right at the hard bump that was my son's misguided head. I stayed in this position for another twenty minutes before giving up for the night, confident that baby heard his mother's rational request to turn around and that he would comply.

The next morning, before waddling to the bathroom for the tenth time, I rubbed the top of my belly searching for that hard bump and hoping it had moved. I searched and searched, but didn't feel the hard bump. *It's not there! No, wait, there it is*, I realized. His head had moved to my side instead of the top of my stomach. *Well, he's moving. He's just traveling at a slower pace— taking the scenic route. There's still time*, I reassured myself.

"There is still time." This phrase is what I heard from everyone—on the phone with my mom, "Oh, there is still time, dear. All my babies turned at the last minute."

"There is still time," my boss said, "My son turned during labor!" There is still time, right? Even though at this point, 97% of babies are in the head-down position.

For the next few weeks, I tried everything. Well, not everything. I did research about chiropractic techniques and ancient Chinese medicine. After some consideration, I decided that I didn't have time or trust in those methods.

I went to the pool and did somersaults, again, and again, and again. I looked like a seal that had lost its way and was looking to get back to the aquarium before the water show began. Okay, I looked more like a whale, but seals are cuter.

I played Disney songs at my vagina so that he might move to the sound. He didn't. Already, a critic of Walt Disney, I guessed.

Every night I laid on the ironing board rubbing my belly in a clockwise motion. Every morning, I woke up and searched for my baby's head, which was always in the same place.

Each week I Googled the number of weeks I was pregnant and questioned if he would still turn. "Thirty-six-weeks pregnant and breech, will he still turn? Thirty-seven-weeks pregnant and breech, will he still turn?" As if Google was some sort of oracle. For the record, it's not.

I found some comfort searching the mommy comments for stories of babies turning at the last minute. I ignored the stories that ended in a C-section. I built up in my head that my body was not only capable of delivering naturally, but was meant to. I already resented my little baby for robbing me of the opportunity to give it at least a shot.

At my thirty-eight-week appointment, the ultrasound technician came in. She said, "Let's see if our little buddy is head down, shall we?" He wasn't. I knew even before the goo hit my belly.

My doctor came in and sat down. It was time to talk about our options.

"Julia, your blood pressure is a little high and your baby is breech. At this point, I would recommend a C-section."

I started my carefully prepared negotiations.

"Can I wait to go into labor naturally and see if he turns?"

"Not with your blood pressure this high."

"Can you try to turn him?"

"Not at this late stage and not with your blood pressure this high."

"Can we at least wait until he's 39 weeks so he is full-term?"

"Yes."

I have never been good at negotiating. She pulled up her calendar on her laptop and we scheduled the day my baby would enter into this world like we were scheduling a brunch date.

"How's Monday, March 17?

St. Patrick's Day? I envisioned him on his twenty-first birthday, lying in a ditch outside of some fake Irish pub in downtown Boston, his red hair, like his father's, sweaty and wet from all the spilled, green-tinted beer.

"Uh, no."

"Wednesday, March 19?"

Hey, that's my grandfather's birthday—he's a grizzly bear of a man, fought in Korea and WWII, loves the outdoors, gives the best hugs, and they call him the Harbinger of Spring.

"Yes, that works."

She typed the appointment into her calendar and sealed all of our fates. She gave me instructions—don't eat after 10 pm and wash with special soap. I was only half listening, waiting until I could waddle to my car and have a good cry. I felt like I had already failed at this whole mother thing. When I got home and my husband found me crying, he tried to console me. "You are a planner. You love scheduling things. Now you can get everything in order before the baby arrives." It helped. Okay, not really.

Everyone told me to do something special the night before the C-section. "Last night before your life changes forever. Go to the movies, go out to dinner." I could barely heave myself out of bed to make it to the bathroom, let alone have the energy and stamina for dinner and a movie. As if my life wasn't already forever altered. We order take-out sushi because at that point, who cared about raw fish and mercury? And damn it, I deserved it. Don't judge.

I slept for a few hours. When I woke up, it was still dark out. I started to cry again. I didn't want to wake Brian so I decided to take a hot shower—and I mean really hot. Again, don't judge. The hot water washed away my tears. I rubbed the pink disinfectant soap on my belly. *Do you still get a birth story if you don't actually give birth?* I wondered. My friend's words suddenly sprung forward in my head, "It doesn't matter how he gets here, just that he does as safely as possible." These words comforted me.

In the hospital, I felt oddly calm and relieved. I would soon meet my stubborn, directionally-challenged son and I would be a mom—his mom. I was surprised to find myself actually getting excited.

The nurse prepared me for surgery. "Little mama, tell me if you feel the cold water." They had just administered the anesthesia.

"What cold water? I don't feel anything."

"Good. We are ready."

Everyone was talking jovially while I was waiting in quiet observation; it was just another day at the office for them. My husband came in and sat by my head. I was so glad to see him. He gave me a kiss on the head and squeezed my hand. Scrubs looked good on him. Before I even realized they had started, my doctor lifted my son above the blue sheet so I could see him.

"It's a boy!"

Yes, we covered that at week twenty, I thought. Then, my husband stood up, shot his arms above his head, and yelled, "Yay!" like he was cheering on the Patriots at Gillette Stadium. I realized that he didn't care what type of birth I had. He was just over the moon to meet his son. How silly I had been.

They brought him close to my head after cleaning him up. "Oh, hello. I'm your mom, Sam. And this is your dad. You could have done worse in the parents department," I said.

I know everyone says that the moment you see your child, nothing else matters. All that worry, pain, and discomfort disappears, and you just instantly love him or her. Well, they are wrong. He looked like a little swollen, pudgy mayor. I didn't think he looked like either one of us. I still felt like he was a little alien. For me, love would come later. But my friend was absolutely right. It doesn't matter how they come into this world, as long as it is as safely as possible. And I do have a birth story. And this is it.

Julia Goddard

Julia Goddard is a public relations professional working in the Boston area. She has ten years' experience in nonprofit fundraising, communications, and marketing. She holds a M.A. in Global Marketing Communications and Advertising from Emerson College and a B.A. from the University of Massachusetts, Amherst. When she's not pitching stories and crafting tweets for work, she enjoys taking nature walks with her husband, son, and two corgis.

Storm Before the Calm

 Lynn Adams

If I kept my eyes shut, I could make it last longer.

Right then, at 6:00 am on Wednesday, September 7, 2005, there was still a chance. It wasn't likely, but it was possible that I was pregnant. I opened my eyes and squinted against the sunlight pouring into my brother's sunroom. I rolled over onto my stomach, the air mattress puckering beneath me. Bruce, my husband, snoozed on. It was still possible for him, too.

There had been sixteen other mornings like this one, when I lay in bed as long as I could so that I could hold onto this feeling. Up until the moment you see a negative pregnancy test, there's still the possibility of a positive one.

"Carol," I'd said the night before to my sister-in-law, trying to sound casual. "I know this is crazy, but I had an IUI the Tuesday before we left, and now it's time to take a test." We could have been in a tampon commercial. Instead, we were using our common vocabulary of infertility, talking about intrauterine insemination (IUI).

"Don't worry," she said. "I can fix you up."

"I don't know what to wish for." That's what I'd said to Carol as I headed up the stairs.

At 5:30 am on Sunday, August 28, 2005, Bruce and I had scooped up our cat, packed up our car, and followed my parents and their cat to Folsom, LA, sixty miles away from our home in New Orleans. We were already worried we weren't going far enough to escape the reach of Hurricane Katrina, but it was too late to make a new plan.

After two nights at our friends' horse farm in Folsom, one of those nights without electricity or running water, Bruce built a road out of tree limbs and we drove out, all of us in the most fuel-efficient car, my Nissan: Bruce, me, my parents, and the two cats.

One cat, the fat one, rode on my lap in his carrier. "You'd better move around a lot," said my mother from the backseat, her hand gripping my shoulder, "or you'll have an embolism like David Bloom in Iraq. That was so sad." She kept her hand on my shoulder for the next mile, patting. We spent the next two nights eating like kings and drinking like winos, staying with generous strangers in Memphis. They were a friend's in-laws, and we'd called from a payphone thirty minutes before showing up.

Then there was a night at a Motel 6 in Knoxville. We'd found a hypodermic needle on the rug before going out for chicken and dumplings at the Cracker Barrel next door. As we burst through the bushes separating the two establishments, a rat skittered across our path. "Is this it for us, from now on?" I asked Bruce.

The next two nights we spent with my aunt and uncle in Dillwyn, VA. We left the skinny cat with them, which they barely noticed, because they already had ten.

We'd been staying in DC for three nights with my brother, Robert, and his wife, Carol. We knew our house had wind damage, but we didn't know if we still had our jobs, or when the mayor would lift the mandatory evacuation order, which ended up lasting six weeks. Our welcome in DC was already wearing out.

Over the previous sixteen months, Bruce and I had taken the same path as lots of couples our age. First we tried to get pregnant by having as much sex as possible. Then I began taking my temperature every morning and recording the results on a graph, in order to pinpoint the single best day of the month to have sex. After having several blood tests, I took a pill called Clomid that made me throw dinner plates. Then there were a few intimate tests and procedures, one of them to make sure my fallopian tubes were open.

Then we did IUI. For eleven days I'd gone into my bathroom, washed my hands, sterilized the counters, and injected myself in the abdomen with the fertility drug Menopur. There were more shots, too, to delay ovulation for a few days and then to trigger it. There were daily blood tests and vaginal ultrasounds. One night only, I insisted that my husband witness what I was doing to get pregnant. He sat on the side of the bathtub, listening to the clink of the little glass vials as I unwrapped them and mixed the medication with saline. He watched me attach a smaller needle to the syringe, so that it would hurt less. Every other time, I was alone in the bathroom, alone in the house, the door locked.

I was doing drugs.

We'd had one failed IUI the previous month, and my husband had tried and failed to conceal his pride about his astronomical sperm count. It was me. I was the reason we weren't getting pregnant, because of my age, thirty-four. There'd been another impressive sperm count that August, and on the afternoon of the twenty-third I'd lain on an exam table, my feet in stirrups, as our reproductive endocrinologist used a turkey baster-like gizmo to insert my husband's sperm into my body. At the time, my husband was five miles away in a meeting. I'd waited the requisite thirty minutes with my nether regions elevated, reading a People magazine. Britney Spears was having a baby shower. Then I'd gone back to work. I was a child psychologist, so I spent that afternoon rolling around on the floor with other people's toddlers.

That summer I had a patient with Down syndrome whose mother had had five miscarriages before becoming pregnant with him. He was a real handful. The chief psychiatrist made an offhand comment in our staff meeting: "Some people just weren't meant to have children."

It haunted me.

I rolled off the air mattress and stood by the door, my hand sweating on the knob. I looked back at my sleeping husband. He had a serious look on his face. I crept next door to the guest bathroom and locked myself in, avoiding the mirror as I unwrapped the test, careful not to pee on my own hand as I'd done before. I closed my eyes and waited as long as I could, trying to get that good feeling back. It was still possible, if only for three more minutes. My chest felt warm, like it always used to feel before tests at school. This was dread. I opened one eye and looked at the stick. There were two lines. It was positive.

On May 15, 2006, our son James was born in New Orleans. My sister-in-law Carol gave birth to twin daughters five days later in DC. People would call our son a "Katrina baby," one of those babies conceived out of panic, relief, or boredom, after the storm. We knew he wasn't, though. Not technically.

I crept back to the sunroom, licking my lips and trying to close my mouth. I sat on the air mattress, making Bruce slide into the void I'd made. I slid beside him and put my hands in his hair. "Bruce," I whispered. "Get a load of this. This is the time. This time it worked." He kept his eyes closed. His smile was beautiful. It made a straight line across his face, his red lips soft and barely turned up at the corners.

Our second child, a daughter, has the same smile.

Lynn Adams

Lynn Adams is a clinical psychologist turned at-home mother who lives in New Orleans with her husband and two children. Her work has appeared in *Salon.com*; *Brain, Child*; and other publications in print and on the Internet.

Bless the Baby, but Fuck all of the Fluids

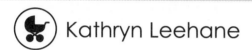 Kathryn Leehane

With three-and-a-half weeks left of my first pregnancy, I lost bladder control. I literally could not stop the pee.

Fortunately, I was sitting on the toilet when it happened. I had just finished peeing for the thousandth time that day and started to wipe when more liquid came out. So I wiped again, and more came out. As I sat there contemplating wearing an adult diaper for the next few weeks, I noticed the tissue was slightly pinkish, not yellow. I gave it a quick sniff and confirmed that it wasn't urine.

Relief at not facing incontinence led to the horror that my water bag was busted. Impossible! I still had three-and-a-half weeks to go! I hadn't packed my hospital bag! I hadn't finished nesting!

I called my husband. Unfortunately, he didn't answer because he was in class, and the reception on campus was deplorable. He had no idea I was even trying to get a hold of him. So I phoned my mother.

"Uh, mom? I think I'm leaking amniotic fluid. At first I thought I couldn't stop peeing, but turns out it's not that. Thank goodness, right?"

"Uh, Kathryn? Hang up the phone and call your doctor. Immediately."

Of course the doctor's office told me to go to the hospital right away.

"I probably shouldn't drive myself, eh?" I asked the nurse over the phone. Apparently I was losing my mind along with my uterus juice.

"Definitely not. Have someone drive you or call an ambulance."

Well, shit. My husband was in class, inaccessible, and wouldn't be home for hours. I called my friend, Carrie, who lived close by. She was about thirty-four weeks pregnant with her third child. She would know what to do.

"Hang tight," she said. "I'll be right there."

I attached a ginormous maxi pad to my underwear, took my dogs outside to go to the bathroom (I couldn't have them leaking all over the house like I was), grabbed my keys, and waited by the door. Slowly dripping like an old faucet with a broken washer.

On the way to the hospital, gushes of neonatal nectar started bursting out. My pad wasn't able to hold all of the fluids. The seat around me became damp.

I kept muttering, "I'm so sorry. The baby balloon wasn't supposed to pop this early." Fortunately, Carrie got us to the hospital quickly. I'm sure it had nothing to do with the pool of womb water that was forming in her car.

When we entered the hospital, the admitting nurse looked each of us up and down. It was probably a site to behold—two very pregnant women standing there at the registration desk. She looked back and forth at each of us and finally asked, "Who's in labor?"

"That would be me," I replied. "I'm not actually peeing, I swear," pointing to my visibly wet maternity jeans.

After they checked me into my room, I tried to reach my husband again, but he still didn't answer. I left a message, "Hey. The baby is busting out a little early. If you're still on-campus, come directly to the hospital. If you're at home, come directly to the hospital. Oh, and sorry about the mess in the bathroom."

The nurse came in to my room, reviewed my chart (noting that I wasn't having contractions yet), and eyed me suspiciously, "Well, we need to run a test to make sure it's really amniotic fluid."

"Well, it's either that or my vagina is crying—really big tears."

As much as she didn't appreciate my humor, I think it was preferable to the gush of sac sauce that came out all over her hands as she put the test strip in my hoo-ha.

My husband and the contractions arrived about the same time. As my labor progressed over the next few hours, the pain became more intense than anything I had ever experienced. I sounded like a myriad of wounded animals dying a thousand deaths as I staggered up and down the hospital halls white-knuckling the handrails along the walls.

The nurse gently suggested I use the birthing tub, as warm water might soothe the labor pains (or at least move the cacophony out of the hallway). My husband led me over to the Jacuzzi tub and prepared the water as I wailed in pain behind him, "Hurry up! OOH-AAH, OOH-AAH I need to relax!"

I finally lowered my hefty body into the tub, closed my eyes, and took a few deep breaths. With the final exhalation, I hurled the entire contents of my stomach into the warm, bubbling water.

The vomit floating around me momentarily distracted me from the labor pain.

The problem then became what to do next. I needed to get out of tub, but I couldn't get up by myself. My husband bravely reached into the amnio–puke soup to help me. I stood there, hand against the wall, trying to catch my breath before the next contraction arrived, dripping and covered in regurgitated food bits. Without a word, my husband proceeded to hose down my enormous naked body.

"Make sure you—OOH-AAH, OOH-AAH get the chunks off of my ass too," I helpfully directed between contractions.

Fortunately the anesthesiologist arrived shortly after my barf bath to take me out of my misery. The next several hours were relatively uneventful. I lay in the hospital bed watching my contractions on the monitor while my husband slept beside me. In the early dawn, the doctors decided it was time to get the real party started so they pumped me full of Pitocin (to help progress labor) and antibiotics (to kill anything they hadn't tested for because I wasn't supposed to be in labor yet).

As we waited for my cervix to open wide enough, back labor had me on all fours on the hospital bed with a nurse firmly rubbing down my back. I was like a naked, screaming, interactive museum display. It was painful and mortifying, but at least I wasn't puking anymore.

Then it came time to push. So I pushed. And pushed. And pushed. In between pushing, one of the nurses exclaimed that my daughter had a lovely head of hair.

"Would you like me to get a mirror so you can see her?" she excitedly inquired.

I had seen enough of my own bodily fluids for a while. "Uh, no."

The doctor explained that my daughter was ready to come out, but she was stuck because my baby gate was too narrow. He suggested an episiotomy to help her escape. I agreed and watched in horror as he whipped out his shiny scalpel. Turns out the epidural wasn't quite strong enough, because I felt that sharp blade slicing my perineum.

"OW-OUCH" I screamed. With my eyes squeezed shut from the pain, I imagined blood was spraying in all directions.

Then my daughter practically shot out of my body along with the rest of the uterine fluids, which splashed audibly on the hospital floor.

My beautiful baby girl had finally arrived. Three-and-a-half weeks early. And dripping with blood and goo.

I know what you're really thinking: *With all of these fluids, I bet she pooped on the table.* Well, we'll never know. I invoked the lesser-known "Don't Ask, Don't Tell" policy during delivery. My husband has graciously agreed to take that secret to his grave.

After my husband cut the cord, one of the nurses coached me through the relatively easy process of pushing out the placenta.

"Would you like to see your placenta?" she brought it over for my inspection.

Relieved not to be expelling or handling any more bodily fluids, I examined it with interest and declared, "Huh. It kind of looks like a flank steak."

Kathryn Leehane

Kathryn Leehane is a writer and humorist living in the San Francisco Bay Area with her husband and two children. Along with inhaling books, bacon, and Pinot Noir, she writes the humor blog, FoxyWinePocket.com, where she shares twisted (and only sometimes exaggerated and inappropriate) stories about her life as a mother, wife, friend, and wine-drinker in suburbia. She is a contributing author to several anthologies, and her essays have also been featured on *BLUNTmoms*, *The Huffington Post*, *Scary Mommy*, and more.

Four Is the Magic Number

 Ashli Brehm

An hour before I started to push my first child out into the world, I was laying in my hospital bed, applying makeup. Labor is that easy.

I checked into the hospital on a Wednesday. I was a high-risk mama, co-managed by a touchy-feely midwife and a down-to-business perinatologist. I was on constant monitoring. I was basically handcuffed to the bed.

There were no leisurely strolls down the halls to peruse the impressive artwork. There was no taking quarters down to the vending machine for a candy bar—I was told these were a necessity on my "what to bring to the hospital" checklist. In fact, there were no candy bars of any type because I was also not allowed to eat. There was no passing go and collecting two hundred dollars. By all accounts, I was basically going straight to labor and delivery jail. Just the experience I'd had in mind when I drafted my seventeen-page birthing plan.

The first order of business was this: a pill needed to be inserted in my lady parts. I was concerned about this process, as the last time I'd let someone stick something in my hoo-ha, I'd ended up pregnant. Okay, not the last time. But at 36 weeks pregnant, the last thing that sounded like a good time was having someone digging for gold in my Girl Friday. But, I had no say in the matter. The human I'd been harboring for eight months and I had reached the point of no return. My placenta had given its eviction notice and the party was underway whether I was ready for it or not. So, pill into the parts. And the big dance would commence.

Except when it didn't.

Because after a round of Cytotec to try to open sesame, a round of Pitocin, a drug intended to cause incredible pain, and another round of Cytotec, my cervix was still as closed up as a Hobby Lobby on a Sunday. Thankfully, we could still do arts and crafts as my midwife had packed a crochet hook. The crochet hook (aka, amnihook), popped me like an errant water balloon, and soon, I had a perma-gush happening between my thighs. My blood pressure was in the 200s and I knew that labor was on like Donkey Kong. Two-and-a-half minutes after the geyser blew, when the contractions began to impose on my perfectly planned labor, I asked, "Can I please talk to someone about pain management?" READ: I want that needle in my back, yesterday.

"Four. That's the magic number," the nurse explained. I needed to get my cervix on board with the number four. In order to get an epidural, which, by that point, sounded like the train I wanted to ride, I had to dilate to four centimeters. *No big deal*, I figured. *I have to be at like twelve already, right*? Um…wrong. At thirty-six weeks with my first labor, my cervix was unrelenting. I was at zero. After two rounds of Cytotec, one round of Pitocin, two-and-a-half minutes with a hole in the bucket, and a partridge in a pear tree, I was at zero. *What the French toast!?*

In lieu of the epidural, I chose what was behind door number two, Fentanyl. I'd got a dose and like clockwork, a half-hour in, mid-sentence, I was knocked out cold. But it wore off thirty minutes later, only to leave me clinging to the railing of the hospital bed, apologizing profusely for being in labor, and certain that I would meet Jesus for breakfast because I was absolutely convinced that the pain would kill me. Three rounds of the narcolepsy inducer and I cried uncle, begging someone to bring in the Jaws of Life to pry my cervix ajar.

At that point, the heavens opened and spilled out rainbows—I was close enough to four centimeters. The minute the anesthesiologist walked in, I wanted to open-mouth kiss the man. I didn't, because I could barely breathe through the pain and so covering my mouth with his seemed like an ill-conceived plan.

As he inserted the needle, he inquired: "Did you know you have scoliosis?" My mind flashed to Lisa Kudrow in *Romy and Michele's High School Reunion* and told the man, as I was cringing in pain, "No sir I've never had scoliosis." He persisted and told me I ought to have it checked out. *Sure.* Right after I get this human out of me you lunatic!

I assured him I'd never failed the test in elementary PE, but he was not to be convinced. Outside of having high blood pressure, a placenta that had gone kaput, and an impending child to care for 24/7, I was now adding scoliosis to my laundry list of woes. *Lovely.*

Eventually, I learned to love the man again. Because epidurals are the nectar of angels. Needle, shmeedle. It made any pain I'd been feeling completely dissipate. The next several hours were a non-event. I laid in the bed. Napped off and on. Performed my newest party trick of poking a fork at my leg to prove to people that I was completely numb. And I applied makeup. I was applying makeup because I decided that I wanted my baby to think I looked radiant the first time he or she saw my face.

And then the word "complete" was shouted from the rooftops. The baby was ready to make his or her grand reveal. The room I had been in for what seemed like weeks, the place where I was certain, twenty-four hours before, that I would meet my fate, morphed into a circus tent. There were lights being pulled out of cupboards, instruments appearing out of thin air, and a bear balancing on a ginormous beach ball. Okay, maybe not the bear. But then, 374 people joined us for the labor. Okay, maybe it was only fifteen. But at the time, as the delivery crew, nursery staff, and NICU staff poured in, it felt as if I was one of the Kardashians. By that point, I didn't care if I pooped all over the delivery room. I didn't care if I had given up my perfect birth in favor of an epidural. I didn't even care if my husband saw my privates become alarmingly public. Nor did I care if a resident wanted to grab some popcorn and watch the birth as if it were a sporting event. I was just ready to see the person pushed out of my business and get a sandwich.

I pushed three times and he made his entrance. A boy! I held him. Then they took him. As I sat there, watching my midwife wave my placenta in the sky and begin stitching up my forever-changed cha cha with the world's largest needle and thread, the nurse approached.

"There are some issues. We think he might have Tracheosophageal Fistula, or T. fistula."

A wha?! I thought.

"He also has an undescended testicle."

Poor little one-nutter.

"And some webbing."

Stop the music.

"He has some webbing? Like, a duck?"

"His fingers are connected."

I lost my shit. *I have scoliosis and now my wee bambino has T. fista-what?* I could handle the testicle business. Two seems excessive anyway. But webbing!? I'd had twenty-six ultrasounds and no one could have told me that my kid had fins? No one had any clue that I was carrying the next Michael Phelps? My mind ran on as they whisked the little man away for ultrasounds. I wanted nothing more than to do a shot of tequila. This was not how everyone said it was supposed to go. You birth the babe, you count their (separate) fingers and toes, wrap them up in a blanket, and you go back to your regularly scheduled program.

Eventually they brought him back. He didn't have T. fistula. He did have webbed fingers. *But that adds character,* I thought.

We arrived on a Wednesday, it was now Friday, and we were the proud owners of our very own person. A 4-pound, 9-ounce person that we were in complete awe of. While I still wanted the shot of tequila, a glass of champagne, and cake, I also just wanted to not let them take him away from me again.

Labor hurt like a beast. It was not easy. My girl parts were definitely torn up about the whole experience. It was scary. Awful. Hilarious. Freaking magical. But I did it two more times and I've never regretted getting to be the conduit for miracles. In fact, for me, of all the things I've ever done, I think it has been the most worthwhile.

Ashli Brehm

Ashli Brehm (pronounced like Brain with an M rather than an N) is the author of her own personal blog BabyOnTheBrehm.blogspot.com and also a contributing blogger at Her View From Home. She is the mama to three boys, and wife to one man, Adam, with whom she is slightly obsessed. She began blogging when her first baby set up shop in her uterus, and now it's a hobby she just can't quit. She was a non-profit gal who is currently a full-time, stay-at-home momma who loves her children and yet, on more than a few occasions, finds herself losing her shit because she just doesn't feel like she can get it right. She has had babies on the brain, and on the Brehm, since 2008, and has been chronicling bits and pieces of her life ever since. Originally a small town Nebraska girl, Ashli and the whole Brehm bunch live in Omaha.

Life's Disgusting Miracle:

A Father's Thoughts on Witnessing Labor and Delivery

 Richard Black

My wife's water broke around one o'clock in the morning and that was the only part of her labor that went according to plan. Now that I think about it; however, I don't remember writing down "have water break" on our birth plan. We called the obstetrician (our OB, as birthing couples in the know call them) who instructed us to head immediately to the hospital. We called our doula who instructed us to ignore our OB as long as we didn't see or feel an umbilical cord. We didn't, so Laura spent the next six hours hopping out of bed to run to the bathroom every fifteen minutes.

Fun fact. When the amniotic sac breaks not all of the fluid is released at the same time. Fluid tends to spurt out as the baby's head bobs up and down. Isn't that something!?

We headed to the hospital and, over the next twenty-five-some-odd hours, the train didn't fall off the rails, it grew wings and launched to fucking Mars.

This was Laura's first pregnancy and most likely her last. It had taken us five years of in vitro fertilization to get to this point and our daughter, the daughter that my wife was carrying, was the last embryo we had available. We were, I feel comfortable saying, as invested as parents can be.

From the moment we discovered Laura was pregnant we planned for our daughter's delivery. We attended classes and made birthing plans. We visited the local hospitals and rewrote our birthing plans. We did, in short, the sorts of things that freaked-out, soon-to-be parents do in an attempt to plan for an event that defies most planning attempts.

Laura decided that she wanted to deliver naturally without the use of Pitocin, an epidural, or even an IV. I thought she was nuts but I understood where she was coming from. My wife wanted to be "present" during her entire labor and delivery. She also wanted what was best for our daughter. The fact that she dislikes needles probably had something to do with her decision as well.

We also requested that staff limit their number of exams which I thought was a little strange until I saw one in action. There really isn't an appropriate male analog for an exam, but if there were it would involve a doctor up to his shoulder in a man's colon while he's suffering from a bout of irritable bowel syndrome.

We showed up at the hospital around 7:00 am to find that after laboring for six hours, Laura's cervix hadn't dilated. Our doula arrived shortly thereafter and made me get my wife a sandwich. By the way, the smartest thing we have ever done was hire a doula. Unless your husband is an obstetrician you should hire a doula and even then you should probably do it anyway. For the record, the second smartest thing I've ever done was get my wife a sandwich.

Fun fact number two. If your doula suggests that you get your wife something to eat she expects your wife to be in labor for a long, long, long, long time.

Laura spent the next eight hours walking around the hall, in various squatting positions, or sitting on a ball. Of course none of our activities did much to widen my wife's cervix, but they had the benefit of giving us something to do to pass the time.

Enter Pitocin, an IV, and an epidural. For those of you who are unaware, Pitocin is a medicine used to induce and strengthen contractions during labor. It turns out that strong contractions are incredibly painful. I've never had one, but after watching my wife go through four hours of them I gathered that they weren't a whole lot of fun. For her effort, Laura's cervix dilated to a whopping three centimeters. She called for an epidural and I looked out the window for signs of the impending apocalypse.

Laura really doesn't like needles. I can't stress that enough. Her relationship with needles is about as amicable as the one between Palestine and Israel, albeit with fewer religious overtones. Her decision to have a needle planted into her spine was my first indication of really just how much pain my wife was in.

Fun fact number three. Some men pass out when seeing a fourteen-inch needle plunged into their wife's back.

While administering the epidural the nurses didn't want me in the room. When I insisted they made me sit on a stool, presumably so my head would have less distance to cover before it hit the floor if I passed out. I felt like the least I could do was watch the procedure and not pass out, which is really what most men feel like doing while their significant others are in labor.

Men are remarkably ancillary to labor. I'm sure we provide some measure of comfort (at least I like to think I did) but when it all comes down to it, our biggest job is to tell the woman to push at a stage in the process when she hardly needs the reminder.

The epidural worked well in that Laura couldn't feel anything from the waist down, which isn't exactly the way I'm told an epidural is supposed to work, but she soldiered on. After undergoing four more hours of contractions, Laura was exhausted and our doula suggested that we try to get some sleep. To my great surprise we did. Laura conked out for five hours and I got a full fifteen minutes because I'm an idiot who cannot remember to turn off his phone. Without Laura to focus on, I became aware of every buzz and ping notifying me that fifteen billion well-meaning but, frankly, unwelcome friends and family members were "just checking in."

how r things going?

my wife is pushing a ten pound child out of her vagina. How r you?

Let us know if we can do anything

can u teleport my daughter to a woman with a bigger vagina?

By 7:00 am Laura's cervix had finally dilated to 10 centimeters and the pushing began. She pushed for four hours and for all of that, and despite my constant reminders, all we could see was the top of our daughter's head. Laura's contractions had weakened and our daughter was stuck.

Fun fact number four. When a bunch of nurses and doctors crowd into the delivery room with your OB, it's not because they want to hang out.

Our OB, a good looking fellow I will call Dr. Sohot, showed up around this point and tried to suction our daughter out of Laura's birth canal. He placed a plunger like device on my daughter's head and pulled hard. Really, really hard. He pulled so hard that when I heard a "pop," I thought that he'd pulled off my daughter's head. Then he did it two more times.

"We're going to have to perform a C-section," Dr. Sohot announced. This prompted my wife, who was on the brink of tears, to ask, "How can you do a C-section when she's so far down?"

Fun fact number five. When a baby is stuck in a woman's birth canal and the OB decides to perform a C-section, he: Pushes. The. Baby. Back. Up. Into. The. Woman's. Uterus.

For better or worse, I didn't witness that particular event. While I was putting on a set of scrubs outside and Dr. Sohot was performing a reverse delivery, Laura was discovering that her sense of touch was the only thing that wasn't dulled by lidocaine.

After an eternity that probably lasted all of four minutes, I was finally allowed to enter the operating room. The first thing I saw was the bottom half of my wife. The second thing was a curtain to prevent Laura from seeing her bottom half, which was completely unnecessary as she wasn't in much of a condition to see anything. My wife was well and goodly looped. In an effort to ease her pain, the anesthesiologist had unwittingly added "being conscious for my daughter's birth" to the pile of things that did not go according to plan.

I spent the bulk of the time during the C-section on the safe side of the curtain and then five, maybe ten minutes later, my daughter Darcy was born. Dr. Sohot pulled her out of my wife like a magician pulling a rabbit out of a hat. He wasn't wearing a cape and he didn't have a wand, but I'm pretty sure he said "TaDa!" and there, at last, was Darcy.

The first thing I remember about seeing my daughter had more to do with my ears. Darcy was not happy about the past 32 hours, and wasn't afraid to let everyone know her thoughts on the matter. I can honestly say that I loved her from the start, and while it would be sweet if I said something about how her wails at the age of four remind me of the day she was born, they don't because barring a serious injury, any four year old who is crying is most likely trying to sucker you into something.

My newborn daughter was shuffled off to a corner of the room to be weighed and poked and prodded, which worked out as my wife needed some attention. Laura handles anesthetics about as well as she tolerates needles. Everything becomes a worst-case scenario, the most dire outcome she can possibly imagine will, in her mind, occur. To add to the fun she also firmly believes that I'm lying to her.

"Is she okay? I can't hear her? I can't hear my daughter," Laura mumbled.

"She's fine honey. Darcy came out screaming. People on the other wing of the hospital can hear her scream."

"You're lying to me. I can't hear my daughter. That can't be my baby," Laura sobbed.

We were on our seventh or eighth round of this when Dr. Sohot broke the monotony.

"This, Mr. Black," he said with the air of someone with something particularly interesting to reveal, "is your wife's uterus." And there above the courtesy curtain, and a full two feet above where it should have been, was, in fact, my wife's uterus. The good doctor then went on to point out Laura's fallopian tubes and a piece of her placenta. "Sometimes we have to take it out in chunks," he added.

"Nifty," I said attempting to mask as much of my discomfort as possible. Before I could really take in Laura's innards, my attention was directed back to my daughter.

"We'd like to test your daughter for a chromosomal abnormality," said an ostensibly well-meaning pediatrician.

"You mean Down syndrome?"

"We're concerned about trisomy 22."

Now that I've had some time to think about the situation I've decided that, at best, this young go-getter was being overly vigilant. At worst he was taking advantage of an emotional situation and attempting to pad our bill with a fairly expensive test. No matter what his intentions, the seed had been planted and I agreed to the test.

As he left the room I tried to focus on my daughter. She had fallen asleep and I realized that Down syndrome or not, I would love her. She was my daughter and my wife had faced a great number of her fears to bring her into the world. I bent my neck to give Darcy a kiss when I overheard one nurse say to the other, "I don't think she has Down's. I just think she looks like her father."

Laura, Darcy, and I were wheeled away a short time later to our room and had a generally restful stay for the duration of our time at the hospital. Laura recovered quickly and after a few days we determined that Darcy did not have Down's.

She does, however, and perhaps unfortunately, still look an awful lot like her father.

Richard Black

Richard Black is a forty-year-old, stay-at-home father with a four-year-old daughter. Before becoming a father, he worked in marketing and public relations and got fired. A lot. He thoroughly enjoys being a parent almost 70% of the time and highly encourages others to do so. His blog is TheUnfitFather.com.

The Elephant Man in My Vagina

 Teri Biebel

A word of advice if you're pregnant and one of your lady lips is bigger than the other and you want to look at your hoo-ha by holding a hand-held mirror down there between your legs: Don't. Don't do it. It's hideous down there. Trust me. The vagina, on its very best day, is not a thing of beauty. But throw in a varicose vein on one side of the meat muffin and you're looking at something that rivals one of the zombies from The Walking Dead. It would scare even Daryl Dixon.

Let me explain. I was about six months pregnant with my second child and woke up one morning and hoisted my gigantic mountain of a belly out of bed and went downstairs for my morning cup of fake coffee. (Seriously, people, what the hell is the point of decaf coffee? No redeeming qualities at all.) After not even fooling myself for a moment that I was actually going to get even an ounce of energy from the decaf, I lumbered up the stairs and into the shower.

As I lathered up and began washing my lady parts, I felt something odd. Almost Hulk-like. Down there. The weird feeling was only on one side of my pubic plaza. The other side felt quite normal. There wasn't really any pain down near my fun tunnel, just a little pressure, and what felt like a lot of skin.

What the hell was happening in my nether-region!? It felt as if one of my lips was hanging down around my knee, and I'm no doctor, but that just didn't seem right. I finished my shower, raised my titanic body out of the tub and dried off. I then made the biggest mistake of my pregnant life: I grabbed a hand-held mirror and saw my actual fur burger for myself.

Oh my God, the horror! It was freaking nightmarish! It was the stuff of Stephen King books and John Carpenter movies. Freddie Kruger would've run away screaming like a little girl had he seen what I saw that day. Jason would've taken the chainsaw to his eyes. It was awful.

I knew that something wasn't right, but I needed a second opinion. Also, why should I suffer the sight of my mutilated meat curtains alone when my husband was partially responsible for making one of the lips blow up like the Hindenburg? I didn't get myself pregnant, right? He helped, so why shouldn't he enjoy the rewards I was reaping?

I called him up to join me in the bathroom. Naturally, me being fresh from the shower and naked so close to the bedroom, he thought I had something fun on my mind. No I did not. I had something completely un-fun on my mind. What was on my mind was my terribly misshapen moose knuckle. And he needed to see it, whether he wanted to or not.

"What's up?" he asked.

"I need you to look at something for me." I replied.

Leaning in, he sensually whispered, "Is that right?" with a tone of impending nookie in his voice. Oh boy, was he ever going to be disappointed.

"Honey, when I show you what I'm about to show you, you may never want to have sex with me again" I said. A confused look came over his face, and I took his hand and led him to the bed. I lay back and said "What the hell is that on my vagina?"

I had never seen what pure terror looks like until that very day, but there it was. The look on his face gave me the impression that perhaps the baby was now residing in the right side of my pink taco instead of my uterus where it belonged. "Oh that can't be good," he said.

"What the hell is it?" I asked as he turned his head to look away. "What's down there? What's wrong with my hot pocket?"

Averting his eyes the entire time, he whispered, "It's like nothing I've ever seen before. We may want to call the doctor."

I did just that and they told me to come right in. Apparently, when you tell them that there seems to be something the size of a six-month old fetus hanging off of your labia like a monkey swinging from a banana tree, they take you seriously. We rushed right over to the office and I put on the lovely, formal paper dress, hoping that the doctor would be wearing his top hat and spats. What a lovely pair we'd be.

The doctor came in, looked down at my over-grown gravy boat and told me it was nothing to be worried about: it was a varicose vein.

Big-lipped-vagina-girl-say-what?

A varicose vein? How does one get a varicose vein on one's cooter? I thought they only occurred on the legs of 600-pound, sixty-five-year-old women? Apparently that wasn't the most right I'd ever been. Because there it was. A varicose vein on the lip of my giant clam. The doctor said it really wasn't anything to worry about. Probably because he didn't have a giant growth hanging off his nutsack! Don't tell me not to worry! There's a third leg growing out of my sausage sheath and pretty soon I won't need a partner in a three-legged race!

Apparently, the technical term for this condition is vulvar varicosities, and they are pretty normal. But that information didn't warm the cockles of my heart or my rocket socket. Knowing that it wasn't the baby taking up residence in my happy valley put my mind at ease just a bit. However, for the next few months the giant vag vein made its presence known every day, mocking me, making me realize that while pregnancy may be joyful, it certainly isn't pretty.

Teri Biebel

Teri is a working mom of two teenage daughters. She is a writer, a ranter, and a fan-girl with a huge crush on Mike Rowe. Her work can be found in the *New York Times* Bestselling book *I Just Want to Pee Alone*, and you can find her on social media and on her blog, SnarkfestBlog.blogspot.com.

Like Father, Like Sons

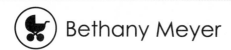 Bethany Meyer

Nothing in this world prepares you for children. Sure, you can babysit. Get yourself a houseplant or two. Maybe go whole hog and get a dog. But none of these things truly prepares you.

Not for the teasing.

Not for the stunts they pull.

Not for the havoc wreaked on your house.

Not for the patience required in the face of their irrational behavior.

Not for the way their hunger strikes at the least convenient time.

Not for their ill-timed sickness that brings your existence to a grinding halt.

Not for the love—primal and fierce—that threatens to swallow you whole.

I was slightly more prepared to have kids than most. Had I spent many years babysitting? Meh. I had a hot spell in the neighborhood when I was 12 years old. Had I owned houseplants? A couple. They all died of thirst. I never did get around to the dog. No biggie.

I had a ringer.

I had my husband.

He accompanied me to every prenatal appointment. Which was mostly wonderful, except for the getting weighed part. I had been a tiny little thing for our entire relationship. During pregnancy, I didn't need the obstetrician's scale to confirm that I was putting on weight like it was my job. Especially not in front of my husband. When the nurse asked me to step on the scale, I pointed my finger at my spouse.

"Turn around," I ordered.

"What?" he asked.

"Turn around," I repeated.

"Why?" he wondered.

"I don't want you to see that number. I don't even want to see that number!"

"You're being ridiculous. You know I love you and I think you're beautiful, and I don't care what that scale says," he said.

"I am carrying your baby," I hissed. "Everything about my existence has changed. Yet everything is the same for you. I'm asking you for one thing. Turn a-fucking-round!"

The nurse gasped, and my husband shrugged. He turned his back as I mounted the scale. She slid the markers around as I whispered, "Hurry up, please, before he looks. Wait, where did he go?"

"I'm over here," he called from somewhere behind me. "Far away from the scale. From the scale...the scale...the scale...the scale..."

"Nice echo," I spat.

I spied the nurse's eyes growing bigger while she looked at the numbers. Then she whipped out a calculator. She cleared her throat and whispered, "Mrs. Meyer, it looks like you've gained twenty-three pounds since your last checkup. The doctor will address this because it's a big gain in a four week period."

I stood on the verge of tears, thinking, *OK, fine, I've eaten ice cream every night, but twenty-three-pounds worth!?*

I stepped off the scale. The nurse and I almost tripped on my husband. His oversized foot was pressed onto the scale.

Twenty-three-pound gain my foot. Er, his foot.

"Gotcha!" he exclaimed, and added jazz hands for good measure.

The baby kicked, and I rolled my eyes.

The stunts he pulls.

While pregnant, I consumed everything in my path. Including my own sense of humor. Which is why I ignored him the entire drive home and for the remainder of the afternoon.

By early evening, I was over it. As we sat down to dinner, he was happy to see me smiling again. But a smile wasn't enough. He wanted to hear laughter.

I scarfed down a taco before he even took his seat. I had just bitten into my second taco as he reached for his first and murmured, "huh, huh, huh, Skywalker."

"What?" I asked as I picked up stray pieces of shredded cheese with my fingers and shoveled them into my mouth.

"Huh, huh, huh, Skywalker," he said as he held his arms out to the sides, pretending to rub an enormous imaginary belly.

"I'm lost." I wiped my mouth with the heel of one hand and reached for a third taco with my other hand.

"Jabba the Hutt! The way you're hoovering those tacos? You're like Jabba the Hutt!" He closed his eyes halfway, held his arms out to the sides again and said, "Huh, huh, huh, Skywalker."

"I'm carrying your baby, sustaining the child as we speak. And you're calling me Jabba the Hutt? Is that what's happening right now?"

"Yes!" he clapped. "Impressions aren't my strong suit, but I think I did that one pretty well, don't you?"

Again, my sense of humor was gone. Sometime in my first trimester I had chased it with a Slurpee and two soft pretzels. So, I stormed immediately out of the room. Then, quickly returned, grabbed two more tacos, turned on my heel, and devoured them in the privacy of my bedroom.

The baby kicked, and I rolled my eyes.

Uh. The teasing.

Time passed as it has the tendency to do. And I got bigger as I had the tendency to do. The size medium maternity clothes were no longer accommodating my pregnant girth, so I went shopping for new—bigger—clothes.

When I returned home, I walked through the front door with my shopping bags.

"Oh, thank god!"

"What?" I asked as I hung up my coat.

"I'm here!" called my husband. "I'm here in the....in the attic... well in the kitchen...well...both!"

I walked towards the kitchen. Where I was greeted by the bottom half of my husband. Doing the running man in midair. But where was the rest of him?

"I need your help! I'm stuck! You know how I'm really good with my hands, but also kinda clumsy? Well, I was in the attic trying to install the recessed lights, and my shoelace got hooked on a screw and I fell between the joists!"

Tiny pieces of drywall fell gently on my head and belly like ceiling snowflakes.

"It appears that your father fell through the kitchen ceiling," I mumbled as I brushed them off my stomach. "Are you okay?" I called in the general direction above me.

"My elbows are really scraped up. And I've been hanging here for a long time waiting for you to come home. How much shopping did you need to do!? I can't hold myself much longer!" he wailed.

"What do you need from me?" I asked his legs.

"Go outside and get my ladder from the shed so that I can get some leverage to pull myself back up."

The drywall pieces were all over the kitchen and a film of white dust covered every surface.

The baby kicked, and I rolled my eyes.

Ooof. The havoc wreaked on the house.

More time passed and one September evening my contractions were more than Braxton Hicks.

"This is it!" we agreed.

I handed my husband the stopwatch, a pad of paper, and a pencil.

"I'll tell you when a contraction starts, and you time how long it lasts," I said. "Then, write down what time it started and how long it lasted for each contraction."

He handed back the stopwatch, paper, and pencil.

"I think you should do this," he said.

"What?" I shrieked. "I'm having the contractions! You're supposed to time them! That's the system!"

"Well, that's a stupid system. It's going to be a long night. Doesn't it make sense that one of us gets some sleep? You'll probably have the baby tomorrow. That means I'll be meeting my son for the first time. I want to be well rested for that." He rolled over, taking most of the covers with him, "Just wake me up if we need to go to the hospital."

The baby kicked, and I rolled my eyes.

Oh, the patience required in the face of his irrational behavior.

My water broke early the next morning. I showered, we grabbed our bags, and we made our way to the hospital. At least, that was the plan. Until he blazed right past it.

"What are you doing?" I demanded. "That was the hospital! I'm in labor right now, we have to go there!"

"I just want to grab something to eat first," he said.

"They have a cafeteria. You can get something in the cafeteria! My water broke. We're going to have a baby!"

"Yeah, I know, but you're not going to have the baby this minute. I just have a hankering, that's all," he said.

"A hankering?"

"Yeah. For a hoagie from Lee's Hoagie House," he replied.

"It's 8 am," I said.

"I know, but I have a hankering! I'm going to get a hoagie before we go to the hospital. I don't want to wait until tomorrow or the next day when I have a hankering! Can you not give me shit about it please?"

The baby kicked, and I rolled my eyes.

Grrrr, the hunger that strikes at the least convenient time.

Thanks to my cervix of steel, labor was longer than we had anticipated. I sat on a Pitocin drip without the comfort of an epidural. So I was feeling—how do you say it? Uncomfortable.

Coincidentally, so was my husband.

My eyes were closed tightly when he shook me to tell me, "I've got big problems."

"What?" I whispered.

"I'm serious. Big problems," his voice was urgent.

I opened my eyes a fraction and peered at him, "What's wrong? Is this about your hoagie?"

He shook his head, "No, that was delicious. I may leave the hospital to get another one because this is taking so long. But," he pointed to one of his eyes, which looked slightly bloodshot, "my eye really itches."

"I don't understand," I replied.

"I hate to say this. But, I think I have pink eye."

I responded the only way I could. By closing my eyes.

"It's really bothering me," he complained. "I don't know what to do. Can you text your pediatrician friend and have her call in a prescription for me?"

"For your itchy eye?"

"I want to be able to enjoy the birth of our baby. But my eye— it's really distracting," he said.

"So, you want me to text my friend while I'm in labor to ask her to call in a prescription for you in case you have pink eye?" I asked.

"That's what I've been trying to say to you," he answered.

The baby kicked, and I rolled my eyes.

Gah! The ill-timed sickness that brings my existence to a grinding halt.

After twenty-six hours of labor and ninety-three minutes spent pushing, our newborn son finally entered the world. He cried in a heap on my chest. My husband leaned his head against mine and reached out his hand to cup our son's tiny feet. His tears fell fast and heavy, down his cheeks, onto his sweatshirt, between our intertwined hands.

I took the first deep breath I'd taken in months. The baby boy whose legs had kicked from within my stomach now stretched those legs against my husband's open palm. *Baby boy, meet your Daddy.* I watched them both with tears in my eyes and a heart fixing to burst.

The love.

That love.

So primal and fierce.

It threatens to swallow you whole.

Nothing in this world prepares you for children.

But my husband? He broke me in.

Enough so that we went through it all again.

And again.

And again.

Bethany Meyer

Bethany contributed chapters to *Tales From Another Mother Runner*; *Brain, Child* Magazine's *This Is Childhood*; humor anthology *I Just Want to Be Alone*, and the *New York Times* Bestseller *I Just Want to Pee Alone*. She resides in Philadelphia, where she raises boys, runs, and writes regularly on her blog BethanyMeyer.com.

Ten Signs You are Entering the Three-Under-Three Club

 Lea Grover

There is a special kind of insanity that causes mothers of babies to decide to become pregnant again.

It happens when your baby is about six or eight months old. The baby is a delight—smiling, cooing, laughing, napping regularly and sleeping through the night. You aren't exactly well rested, but Stockholm Syndrome has set in, and you are over the moon about your beautiful bundle of joy. Distant memories, or maybe even only bad dreams, are those sleepless nights of cluster feeding and colic. The indignities of pregnancy have become myth and rumor. You are a radiant, glowing goddess—Gaia personified. The idea of bringing another little angel into your family seems both obvious and easy.

So, you get pregnant. Suddenly you realize that you'd completely forgotten that it takes ten months to make a new baby, and your little one won't be the perfect angel in your arms all that time. As the pregnancy progresses, and your body suddenly bloats, disgusts you, and swells, you realize you must continue caring for a little person through the entirety of a second pregnancy.

In a haze of constant exhaustion, confusion, and desperation, you survive the pregnancy. Now you have a newborn and a toddler—totally different animals to be certain. And somehow, it almost meets your expectations. Your one year old (or one and a half year old) is still content to snuggle in front of the television while you fade in and out of consciousness, Daniel Tiger entertaining your oldest and a grunting newborn at your breast. But, again, the new baby grows. The toddler grows. They love each other, and their love makes you feel, again, like the embodiment of glorious motherhood. So, again, as the baby begins to explore the possibility of crawling, is sleeping through the night, and laughing at the antics of their older siblings ... you fall into the madness.

You get pregnant a third time.

And then the illusion shatters.

This is no first-time pregnancy. No, this is your third time around this carousel. No more is this keeping pace with a crawling, tottering toddler as you chew ginger and sip decaffeinated herbal tea. No, this is something different.

This is your induction into the Three-Under-Three Club. And here are ten ways you might identify yourself as a member:

1. You have found a size of diaper that will barely fit on your potty training toddler, but that you can still use on your younger kid in a pinch.

2. You have stains on your shirt that could be toddler poo, your vomit, or baby food, and you are both too tired to care and out of clean laundry.

3. You've spent more than one naptime hour standing in front of the open fridge, crying and shoveling chocolate frosting into your mouth with your bare hands.

4. You find yourself watching minivan commercials online, hastily shutting down the browser and clearing your cookies whenever your husband comes into the room, more comfortable with the idea he thinks you're

watching porn than drooling over automatic doors and built in vacuum cleaners.

5. Your desire to live on nothing but chocolate milk and Nutella sandwiches has made you your toddler's personal hero.

6. People at the grocery store see your belly and don't congratulate you. Rather, they give you pitying looks, and avoid you as though you're stricken with Ebola instead of a fetus.

7. You are looking forward to delivering the baby, not to get it out of your belly, but for a three-day "vacation" at the hospital.

8. Your maternity clothes are your regular clothes.

9. The idea of sending your kids to college in diapers and letting them figure it out for themselves has a lot of appeal.

10. You already have a shortlist of names picked out, "For the next one."

That's right, Stockholm Syndrome can set in before you've managed to squeeze baby number three through your lady chute, and despite drowning in diapers and the fact you probably still have the taste of Tums in your mouth, you can't imagine that this is *it*. The fact of the matter is that before you're *really* in the club, you already know. The more children in the house, the more love there is to go around.

And as your excited ovaries seem to whisper in your ear, isn't that worth a few decades of exhaustion and insanity?

Lea Grover

Lea Grover is a writer in Chicago. She scribbles about sex-positive parenting, marriage after cancer, and vegetarian cooking on her blog, BecomingSuperMommy.blogspot.com.

Her publications include *My Other Ex: Women's True Stories of Leaving and Losing Friends, Motherhood: May Cause Drowsiness, Discovering True: The #NoMoreShame Project*, and *Listen To Your Mother: What She Said Then, What We're Saying Now*. When she isn't revising her upcoming memoir, she can be found singing opera, smeared to the elbow in pastels, or complaining/bragging about her children.

Hold Up Your Hold Up, She Needs a Burrito

 Chris Smyrl

My wife and I have lived in Albuquerque, New Mexico, for about twenty years. You may not know this, but in New Mexico the chili pepper is king. While I am not as much of a partaker of the chili as much as native New Mexicans, I can understand their one-minded cravings for them. What I don't tend to understand is their need to put chilies into any and every dish they can imagine. Some are actually surprisingly good, and some are just ludicrous. Green chili ice cream anyone? Chocolate with some red chili? No, I think I will pass, thank you.

The chili I refer to is not the kind that comes out of a can with a cowboy face and includes hamburger and beans. It is also not really much like the little cans that you open and drain and are labeled hot, medium, or mild. I'm talking about actual chili peppers fresh from the vine, or air-dried and rehydrated later. The green ones are most often flame roasted in a turning drum, and have a distinct flavor. My wife loves this variety in particular. I enjoy the red ones; I prefer their flavor, though they are sometimes so much hotter.

My wife tends to enjoy the "farther side of chili" and by that I am talking about green-chili-flavored cookies, candies, and other foods that are a bit more unusual. Like so many in this state, she gets unbearable cravings for these chili foods. This became magnified by several degrees during her pregnancy. Chilies were one of her main cravings.

One of her chili cravings happened at my parent's house. We had just finished a dinner that included zero chilies. She was in need of a chili fix. We were all in that state where you get very full and are just about on the verge of sleep. I wish that I had been a bit more clued-in and mentally alert; I might have known what my wife was about to get up to.

She announced finally that she was going to make a quick run down to the corner to get a burrito with some green chili and she would be back in a few minutes. It wasn't too late, it was a quick trip, and we live in a pretty quiet part of Albuquerque with little reason to worry. I, like the bad, lazy husband I am, let her go on her chili quest alone. After all, she had done several trips like this on her own in the middle of the night without waking me up or letting me know she had left, and all had gone well. I figured she would be just fine.

Dulled by our post-supper stupor, after a time, it occurred to my parents and I that my wife had not returned. Naturally, we began to worry. I called my wife, but my calls were going unanswered. I grabbed the car keys, and started toward the door to see if I could find her.

As I was going out the door, I was surprised to see her walking toward the house carrying a bag of burritos in her hand and a strange look in her eye. What should have been a ten-minute trip had taken twice as long. We were all pretty curious about why it had taken so long. But, pregnancy cravings being what they are, we had to wait as she finished the last burrito out of the bag.

When she finally filled us in, what a strange ordeal it was.

The drive down was nothing special; the parking of the car was no big deal. But when she approached the door to the restaurant, focused only on what she was going to order, she didn't notice the young man standing lookout at the door. His partner was in the process of robbing the place at gunpoint. Not at all aware of what was going down inside, my wife walked up to the door, opened it, and bumped pregnant belly first into a gun muzzle pointed at her by a very confused teenager.

She told my parents and me, "I looked down at the gun, looked at the wide-eyed kid, and said, 'Hmmm!'" Then she reached down, grabbed the gun gently, and pointed it to the side as he stood there dumbfounded. She grabbed his shoulders, turned the young man sideways, and walked up to the counter where the older robber was conducting his business. The second accomplice was struck dumb as she nudged her way up to the frightened store clerk who was shaking.

Let's take stock. There are two extremely confused robbers, probably even more confused employees, all staring at this mad pregnant woman who just shoved herself into the middle of their situation—and placed an order for burritos.

The employee did, indeed, take her order, and at some point during the order-taking process the two thieves must have just given up trying to make sense of what was going on and just walked outside and continued on down the road. No money was lost from the store, and no one was hurt, which was a very wonderful thing considering how it all could have gone down. Basically, the restaurant came through unscathed due to a pregnant woman's craving for chilies.

When she told the story back at my parent's house, we sat there with eyes wide, retroactively frightened for her safety, the baby's safety, and feeling extremely guilty for not going with her. She just leaned back on the couch and entered the sleepy/lazy food stupor we had all been a part of just moments ago.

I am so thankful that this frightening story ended well and no one was hurt. It all could have gone so much differently. God was watching her and my unborn son that day, and the passing of time has erased our alarm. We all smile and chuckle a bit at the woman who would be turned aside by no one or anything in search of a burrito.

Chris Smyrl

Chris Smyrl has always liked writing and literature-related things. In fact, he was raised by two parents that were both English majors. Chris works as a Dental Lab Technician, which gives him some leeway to use his creative side to earn a living. He's married to a lovely wife and has a 7-year-old son who makes him feel stupid half the time because he is so smart. Chris also shares his home with two large dogs, a cat, a rabbit, and many fish.

I Never Planned on Being a Parent

 Sarah Bregel

At the time I turned twenty-four, the only thing I was nursing was a half a dozen vodka martinis and inevitably, a hangover. But by the end of the year, I had a full-time milk guzzler attached to my ever-expanding chest. This had not been in my plans for the year, but then, I was never much for plans.

I've always been a person who does things in extremes. I partied hard. I enjoyed the high highs of life which meant that sometimes I had to dig my way up from the low lows. So, it would only be fitting that when it came time for me to get knocked up, I'd be unmarried, underemployed, and under the influence. Motherhood would knock me off any high horse I'd ever ridden on. But for me, the work of it came early and it stayed late, like I always had.

It is for this reason that getting pregnant was the best and worst thing to ever happen to me. It was the worst because it altered everything I thought I wanted for my life—freedom, excitement, and spontaneity. It was the best because I eventually found out I didn't need those things. But the road to get there was hard, harder than I had thought it would be.

Just a week after taking the test (the test which seems to have only one question but really has hundreds: Where will we live? Can I handle this? Will we be okay? Will I make a good mother?) I was hit with the most attention-demanding nausea of my life. Every day was a battle. Getting out of bed was pure pain. No matter what I'd do to stave off morning sickness, I'd always end up on the bathroom floor for hours upon hours. Finally, I'd move to the couch, I'd bring a bowl, and there I'd stay.

Everything in my life shut down. It was as if someone was trying to tell me to make a clean break. "Leave the rest behind. There's no room for it now. This motherhood thing is gonna get ya." That god-awful nausea, I wouldn't wish it on my worst enemy. But maybe in some ways throwing up my stomach lining for the better part of a year needed to happen to me. Maybe it made my first year as a mother less gut-wrenching because I'd already purged up so much of my past life. Maybe it was my detox, my saving grace. Maybe at the time I delivered, most of the old me was already gone.

For me, pregnancy was hard and terrifying. I'm not sure if it's like this for most people, but it was for me. I didn't eat pickles and ice cream. I ate toast and peanut butter, maybe mashed potatoes, or something that might, hopefully, maybe stick to my stomach. I didn't take the classes or read the baby books. I figured everything would turn out the way it was supposed to (again, not big on the planning).

As my hips grew wider and I peed a little more every time I sneezed, I started to wonder what pregnancy was like for people who actually did plan to be parents and who mapped out every step of the way once they saw that pink plus sign. I'd never so much as thought about being a mother or really knew if I wanted to be one. I wondered how much easier the people who'd desired motherhood for years and years might have it than me, how much more graceful their transitions to being a parent would be than my own.

Over the years, one by one, I've watched my group of friends become parents, each time picking color schemes for the nursery, posting sonogram pictures on the internet, and reading a thousand books about parenting. Most of them have been around babies by now, have a handful of parent friends, a few babysitters on speed dial, and a college savings plan (whatever that is). But the funny thing is that regardless of how we all came to be parents (differing ages, preparedness, and incomes), we now are all in the same exact boat. And we're all up the creek without a paddle.

It took me many years and watching so many meticulously plan their parenting ventures before I really got it—planning for parenthood is an oxymoron. While I didn't have a house, a picture perfect nursery, a family-friendly car or church group that was going to be running over with lasagnas, none of that really mattered. Yes, it is wonderful to have support in your parental journey, but all the rest is peanuts. It turns out, I was no less prepared than anyone else when the shit hit the fan. Or, when my vagina ripped open and a human life came pouring out.

If I had to do it all over again, become a parent for the first time, I'd do it a lot differently. I've made so many mistakes. But I can't say there's much I'd do to prepare. Maybe I'd practice walking quietly or sitting in a chair under a warm bag of water and not moving a muscle, or seeing how long I could go without peeing. I guess I could practice typing or doing dishes with one hand, too, because those are the skills I really need to improve upon.

But the truth is, only being a parent has taught me how to be a parent, and I'm a huge work in progress. While I wish there were a manual to crack open in the middle of the night when I've been up for the past three, there isn't. More than any other journey of my life, right now, I'm putting in the legwork. No,

I was not prepared for parenthood, not in the slightest, but I don't think that's what matters. As far as I can see, none of us are prepared. All I can do is the same as anyone: strive to grow, take deep breaths and keep moving forward.

Though by my own admission, my introduction to motherhood was clumsy, I now have an almost five-year-old daughter and I'm endlessly grateful for the way she bulldozed into my life and, at the time, destroyed it all.

Sarah Bregel

Sarah Bregel is a writer, yoga teacher, feminist, and deep-breather based in Baltimore. The birth of her first child in 2010 led to the birth of her writing career when she realized no one wanted to talk constantly about birth, babies, or the messy business of being a mom. So she started a blog. She has since written for *The Huffington Post, XOJane, The Washington Post, Babble, Scary Mommy, Mommyish, SheKnows Parenting, Mutha Magazine,* and *Mamalode*. She lives with her husband, daughter, and baby boy, and blogs about the endlessly terrifying journey of motherhood at TheMediocreMama.com.

Feet in the Air

 Emily Ballard

It started with my feet in the air.

We'd been home from our three-week Corsican honeymoon for about five days, and it was time. I wanted a baby and I wanted it yesterday and if post-sex-feet-in-the-air was the way to make it happen, I was game.

My husband found me in the living room.

"What are you doing!?" he laughed.

"Hopefully getting pregnant." *Obviously.*

Ⓐ Ⓑ Ⓒ

A few weeks after we were married we moved into a new apartment because it's always wise to make major life-changes in close proximity to one another.

It was in that new apartment, while taking a break from unpacking boxes of dishes and spices and Ball jars full of grains and seeds that I peed on a stick, screamed, and thought I might explode.

Because I was pregnant. Because there were two lines!

I also thought I might explode because I'd been fairly certain that I was going to have a really hard time getting pregnant. I'd only had a handful of periods throughout my teen years, and every doctor I visited told me to "just go on the pill." Why bother finding out what's really going on? That'd be preposterous.

A few years before we got married, once we'd firmly settled into the hills of Western Massachusetts, I sought out the opinion of a naturopath. He asked me a few questions that included the words "estrogen" and "progesterone." My answers sounded something like, "I don't know what you're talking about. Really. Like, at all." The nurse drew some blood and a week or so later we were in business: low progesterone levels. I started rubbing an expensive cream onto my arm the next day, and soon I got my period. After years and years of "just go on the pill," I was thrilled.

Okay, back to the double lines. I was relieved. So, so relieved. I was more excited than I'd ever been about anything in my life. Growing up, I was the kid who'd hand my mom the Mother's Day gift I'd made her the second school let out—waiting for Mother's Day was an impossibility. Delayed gratification? What the hell is that?

I needed to tell someone immediately.

Instead, I waited for what felt like nine-and-half hours. Okay, it was more like two, but who's counting? I planned to play it cool. *"Oh, hey, babe. How was your day? Oh, mine? Fine. I unpacked, as you can plainly see. Oh, let's see, what else?"* I would not freak out. For once, I was going to be nonchalant, catch him off guard, and surprise him with my calm.

Uh, huh.

Right.

I heard my man's work boots on the front porch and when the doorknob turned I assaulted him. There was nothing calm or collected about me.

"LOOKATTHISLOOKATTHIS, BABE, LOOKATTHIS!"

I was shoving the peed-on pregnancy test in his face.

He stared at me.

"Babe, aren't you excited!? Look!"

"I don't know what that is." He tried to walk through the door.

What? How can you not know what this is? Look at my face. My face will only ever look like this when—

"I'm pregnant!"

He shut the door.

"What?" he said, mystified.

"I'm pregnant."

"*What?*"

"I know."

"Wow."

"I know."

My pregnancy was lovely: I never vomited, though I really, really wanted to. When I wasn't falling asleep standing up, we planned a homebirth. I cursed when he hugged me too tightly because my breasts felt like two giant bruises. I was temporarily convinced that the bite of raw cookie dough I'd been unable to resist was going to kill my child.

As you can see, I was a typical first-timer.

As soon as we hit thirty-six weeks—the safe-to-have-a-homebirth zone—I was confident the baby would be here any day. Every time I made plans, I wrapped things up with, "So, I'll see you then, unless the baby comes!"

When we got to forty-two weeks, and then to forty-three weeks, well past our due date (which should really be called a "Do You Have Any Real Idea When You Got Knocked Up?" date), I became despondent. Logically, I knew that this child could not live inside of me forever, and I was adamant that unless there was a legitimate medical problem, we weren't inducing.

And so we waited.

My midwives came to the house daily to listen to the baby and count the seconds between its movements. Looking back, they were the sweetest, simplest days: me, tasked only with lying on my side and maintaining this tiny life, belly bursting out before me.

As we neared the end of week 43, one of my midwives sat me down. "Are you scared of something? Are you sad? If there's anything in you that's holding this baby in, let's get it out."

I wept.

I wept because four years earlier my father had died and would never get to meet his grandchild. I wept because what if something went wrong and I needed a C-section? I wept because the anticipation was just too much.

I wept because I was done.

Ⓐ Ⓑ Ⓒ

Hours later, in the middle of the night, labor began.

I labored through the night and all of the next day. I followed the sage advice of one of my midwives—"don't give the contractions any more attention than you absolutely need to"— and managed to file our taxes and go out for lunch.

"It's a girl," I stammered as my husband drove us quickly home from town that afternoon. Things were accelerating. My adrenaline was pumping. "I've been telling myself it's a boy because I want to be prepared for it not to be a girl. But it's a girl. I know it."

We arrived home around 4:00, and when my water broke, around 4:30, that was that; the four-and-a-half hours of active labor it took to bring our child from inside to out are a blur of intensity, power, self-assuredness, and don't-you-dare-touch-me.

At 8:59 pm, right when I thought things couldn't crescendo any higher, a human being shot out of my body.

I didn't push once.

Just like that, I was a mama.

"Hi," I said. "Hi, baby."

"She's beautiful," someone said.

Wait, what?

"Wait, is it a girl? Did someone check?" It had been at least a minute or two since this small person had emerged, and hearing "she" made my heart beat faster.

"No, I didn't check. Did you check? No?" midwives and a new father asked each other.

So we checked.

And just like that, I had a daughter.

The midwives stayed to help me get cleaned up. I took a shower with one of them sitting in the bathroom to spot me; passing out after giving birth is not unheard of, the notion of modesty laughable.

They weighed our girl. They watched us nurse. They brought me food.

"You were wonderful. She's beautiful. We'll see you tomorrow."

Wait, what?

They're just going to leave me here? Don't they know I just had a baby?

They must have seen my terror. "You'll be fine," they said. I was dubious. I'd never had a baby before. They were experts. They couldn't just leave.

I heard the front door click.

I looked around my bedroom.

It was a different bedroom.

I looked down at my daughter.

"Hi," I said.

"Hi, baby."

Emily Ballard

Other than diving continuously and often irretrievably into her own head, Emily Ballard likes to spend her hours with her two truly lovely children and her how'd-I-get-so-lucky? husband. They live in Western MA, in a pocket of pure, gorgeous goodness. Emily collects tattoos, each a reminder of important things—love and grief, the seconds she has here, alive. She likes to think about her place in the Universe, and then sometimes gets distracted and ends up on the People website. She gets a little (a lot) crazy for good food. Emily believes in telling our secrets, taking up space, and owning the hell out of our stories. You can find her at EmilyBallard.com.

How Leap Year Ruined My Birth Plan

 Meredith Napolitano

My first child had a delivery that made many a mom hate me. This wonderfully compliant girl arrived at exactly forty weeks and one day. I arrived at the hospital, received an epidural, and birthed a baby girl in under two hours. Quick, uneventful, successful.

See? You hate me. But don't worry, it won't last.

It seems my second child was conceived with the notion that her mom must not be allowed to develop confidence. This would not be a repeat experience.

My first baby was by the book from conception to delivery, but number two put me through the paces. My first trimester was a haze of nausea and dizziness, and once that was over, I experienced near constant Braxton Hicks contractions and ultimately was given the charmingly named diagnosis of "irritable uterus".

I may have been carrying another girl, but it was clear that she and her sister were nothing alike. This baby had been put on earth to make sure that I'm aware that I truly have no control.

Now, in addition to all the contractions, baby two was breech. We waited for her to turn. We encouraged her to turn. But as little as she was, she was stubborn. My midwife suspected that because she was so little and so content, any attempts to manually turn her would most likely result in her flipping herself again. So, a C-section was scheduled for my thirty-ninth week—assuming I made it that long (with how irritable my uterus was, there was not one doctor who thought I'd be making it to my due date).

Honestly, I wasn't all that disappointed. You see, number two was scheduled to arrive on February 28, 2012, and that date scared me. Because what was on tap for the day after February 28, 2012? Not March 1. Not this time. February 29. I did not want a Leap Baby. Not one itty-bitty bit.

A leap baby was not part of my plan. No matter how cool random people thought it was, I didn't want any part of it. I didn't want to worry about when we'd celebrate her birthday. I didn't want to have to override every drop down Internet menu that didn't include 29 as an option once you'd selected February. And I really didn't want to doom a kid to a life of answering stupid questions.

Hardee har har, are you sure you can drive? You're not sixteen! You're four!

Hey, do I have to get you a present? You don't have a birthday on MY calendar this year!

With a planned C-section due to a breech baby, I could have it on absolute authority that she would have a birthday that would appear on the calendar every year. *I had control.* I had a plan. I scheduled childcare, lined up friends and family to help with my toddler during the recovery period, and breathed a sigh of relief.

During the third trimester, people focus on different things, trying to grasp on to just a little bit of control over a world that's about to be changed. Some women clean or cook obsessively. Some read every book on breastfeeding and infant sleep and childcare until they have every theory memorized. Some women fixate on finishing the perfectly designed, furnished and well stocked nursery. Some focus on planning for the perfect delivery, outlining every last detail and possibility in a birth plan.

I fixated on the date. The nursery wasn't finished, the house wasn't pristine, I wasn't through gathering the baby gear from number one, and I didn't have a birth plan. But I had one, crystalized focus. **This baby would not be born on Leap Day.** I was obsessed. And now, with a planned delivery date, I was in control.

I went to my last appointment pre-surgery, and the midwife listened and felt around. Something hadn't felt right, so she popped in to see if the ultrasound tech was free.

That little girl had flipped. She'd flipped, without my feeling a thing, at thirty-nine weeks. There was no reason for a c-section.

I was shocked. The midwife was shocked. The ultrasound tech was shocked. There she was, perfectly positioned for takeoff, looking like she didn't have a care in the world.

We canceled the c-section to let nature take over.

My control slipped away.

And time ticked on.

February 23? No baby.

February 25? No baby.

February 27? No baby.

I saw my doctor on February 28. She was so surprised to see me. How funny! They never thought my irritable uterus would tolerate its occupant this long!

I told my doctor, with a degree of irritability to match my uterus, that I was not having a baby on Leap Day. No. Not happening. I didn't want a Leap Baby. We were going to do whatever we had to do to keep this baby in for the next twenty-four to forty-eight hours. March would suit us just fine.

She gave me that laugh that feels so patronizing to full term pregnant women and told me that babies come when they're ready. No promises, but she felt pretty confident that I'd be getting my wish. For all the contractions that I was having, I wasn't dilated at all. I wasn't effaced. Go home and relax.

How can I relax when tomorrow is Leap Day?????

February 29, one day after my due date, I woke up feeling off.

No. No no no no no no. I was not off. I was fine. I'd been contracting for the past five months. Sure, these were a little … different, but I wasn't screaming with pain.

My husband, logical man that he is, suggested that "just for fun," we call his mom to hang out with our toddler and just "check in" with the doctor. I agreed under the condition that we get sushi on the way there. I mean, I wasn't having a baby. If I was going to leave the house, it was going to be for sushi, not to have a Leap Baby. I was completely and totally willing to rationalize raw fish. I was not willing to rationalize that the baby would be born on Leap Day. I was – ouch – in – OOOOOH – *control DAMMIT*.

One doctor's visit and a maki combo lunch later, I learned that I was, in fact, in labor. My contractions were frequent, but I was moving around and talking through them. This was looking like a long, gradual labor. Or maybe even false labor. I was really fine to go home.

I was back in control.

Slightly before dinner, despite my vigorous denials and attempts to keep this control of the birth date, my husband called the doctor again, since the contractions were now definitely within the parameters of when any sane woman who was 40 weeks pregnant should get herself checked. This time, the doctor decided that instead of the office, I should probably head into the hospital.

I was back out of control.

Six o'clock. We got to the hospital.

Seven o'clock. They sent me home.

And I was back in the driver's seat.

Sure, I was already 3 cm and had a history of fast labor. Sure, I was having contractions every four minutes. But I was just tolerating these things too darn well. They had me walk around the hospital for about an hour and ultimately decided that I should go home, sleep in my own bed, and plan on coming in early the next morning.

Now if I were a *rational* full term pregnant woman in active labor, I would have said no. I would have said that I was contracting, and that my older daughter had come in like a tornado—a lot of calm nothingness before a burst of intensity and immediate destruction, errr, childbirth.

But I wasn't having a Leap Baby! I would *absolutely* go home. I repacked my bag, pocketed the "very mild" sleep aid I was provided, and practically skipped home to wait for my **March** baby. Well, as much as a woman in active labor can skip. Which is not at all.

At eight o'clock, I tucked my big girl into bed, took my sleeping pill, and got ready to relax and count down until March. My contractions were holding steady at four minutes. *I win.*

Nearly three hours later, I was still trying to drift off without success. My husband, who had been hovering, asked if he should go to bed try to get a few hours of sleep in. Sure, I was still contracting, but everything was holding steady and the midwife had been pretty sure we'd be fine until morning, after Leap Day had ended. Go to bed. She said we'd be fine. WE WOULD BE FINE. *I WIN!*

At eleven o'clock all hell broke loose.

Suddenly, every four minutes turned into one endless, everlasting, contraction. Talking and breathing turned into one ridiculous moan. My husband, who had just started his deep snoring, shot out of bed and started putting my shoes on.

After about fifteen minutes of trying to reason a completely irrational woman in labor into the car, he called the midwife, who told us she'd be waiting and that it looked like I'd be getting my wish. We were about thirty minutes from the hospital and forty-five mintues away from midnight on the first day of March.

I'm winning, dammit, I'm winning, I'm in control....

About fifteen minutes into the ride from Hell I felt a pop, a quick release, and then intense pressure.

Me: I think my water broke.

Husband: I'm already speeding. Do I just hope that if I get pulled over they follow me to the hospital?

Me: I think I have to push.

Him: Okay, then.

We arrived at the hospital around 11:40. Twenty minutes. Twenty minutes until March. Twenty minutes until I didn't have to worry about the date. There was no way I wouldn't make it.

We hustled down the hall with the valet chasing us and an admitting person from the ER jogging and asking questions like, "*Religion? Pediatrician's name?*" We nearly knocked over a group of med students who stopped and stared at the pregnant lady both screaming in pain and asking if it was midnight yet. We made it upstairs and my midwife bustled us into triage.

Me: I'm ready for my epidural. Right now.

Midwife: You're crowning

Husband: So what can we do for pain relief?

Midwife: She's going to have this baby. That will be her pain relief.

Me: Noooooooo.....

No labor room. No gown. No monitors. No more waiting.

At 11:47 pm on February 29, I had my new baby girl.

I have a Leap Baby.

I have a spunky, stubborn, doing it my way, feisty three-year-old girl with a unique personality to match her unique birthday. We celebrate her birthday on the last day of February (since she was born on the last day of February), and, though we get our share of dumb jokes and ridiculous questions, I'm usually prepared for them and I've never *officially* lost my cool with anyone. And next year, when her fourth birthday actually falls on her "real" birthday she will have one kickass celebration of how special she really is.

That kid leapt into the world on a day meant for leaping, and taught me that no matter what I may have thought, I really have no control.

Meredith Napolitano

Meredith Napolitano is a former teacher who made the move to stay-at-home mom in 2012. Meredith began writing shortly after this transition, initially as a way to continue having adult conversations without bombarding her friends with her daily anecdotes. She shares those daily anecdotes along with reflections, silly stories, and moments that become memories, but mostly, she writes about finding the balance between her roles of "Meredith" and "Mommy." Meredith's writing has been featured on many different sites including *The Huffington Post*, *Scary Mommy*, *Circle of Moms*, and *iVillage*. Her stories have been published in several anthologies, including *I Just Want to Be Alone*, *My Other Ex*, *Clash of the Couples*, and *Motherhood: May Cause Drowsiness*. When she's not fulfilling her roles as homeschool teacher, chauffeur, dance mom, housekeeper, cook, boo-boo kisser, and lost item locator, she's connecting with other moms on social media. You can find her on FromMeredithToMommy.com.

Water, Water Everywhere and Not a Drop to Drink

 Christina Antus

My journey into motherhood started with amniotic fluid.

With both pregnancies I wondered where and when I'd go into labor. Would my water break? If so, where would it happen? When would it happen? How would it happen? What would it be like?

I envisioned waves of fluid washing away innocent bystanders and barking dogs. Trash cans sailing down a river of water through the gutter, while Bobby Darin's version of *Somewhere Beyond the Sea* played in the distance.

I was so worried about this that near the end of my second trimester I started carrying a trash bag around in my purse and vehicle's glove compartment. Just in case. I certainly didn't want to ruin my car upholstery, and in the event a kind person offered me a ride to the hospital I didn't want first impressions to start by marking my territory all over their Italian leather interior.

Before I go any further, I'd like to state for the record that the whole expression: "My water broke," is a little ridiculous. Your water doesn't break. It's your amniotic sac that breaks. So, in truth it should be expressed as: "Breaking your sac," because that's what's really going on.

Anyway, sac breaking doesn't happen to every woman. Some women go into labor with their amniotic sac intact and it's pretty common for a doctor to break it before delivery—that means they pop your sac like a balloon. But they don't use a thumbtack. Or their teeth. At least I'm pretty sure they don't. Mostly sure.

I read that only about 14% of women actually experience an academy award-winning gush. And a small percentage of those women are, in fact, acting in movies, and aren't really pregnant. For those it does happen to off screen, it's often anticlimactic. Instead of a rush of water like a fire hose has just been turned on in your pants, a lot of women experience a small, unimpressive leak. Whatever that means. Truth is, at the end of the last trimester, it's kind of tough to tell the difference between an amniotic leak and accidentally peeing a little in your pants.

My water broke with both of my pregnancies. And each time it was different, but nothing like the movies.

During my first pregnancy I felt a snap and thought, "Well, that was weird." Ten minutes later my pants were wet. So, I did what any idiot would do. I changed my pants, put on a panty liner, and went back downstairs to finish my burrito.

Ten minutes later, my pants were wet again. "Maybe you just wet your pants," my husband said. It was a good point; after all it wouldn't have been the first time during this pregnancy that happened. So, I put on my last pair of sweatpants, another panty liner (I'm a slow learner), and went about my evening.

Ten minutes later there was a gush. I wouldn't have been at all surprised if the panty liner had sailed right out of my pant leg in search of the great white whale. Obviously this distorted my overall opinion of panty liner absorbency and sent it to the top of the list of useless methods.

This time everything came out but a baby. Gallons of fluid preceded a large gelatinous blob of what looked like, well, a large gelatinous blob. I could only presume it was a mucous plug because what else could it be? It turns out, those things aren't really an effective plug. Maybe they are for keeping infection out, but not for keeping gallons of fluid in. It's like trying to stop a leak in the Hoover Dam with a piece of snot.

By the time I got to the hospital, I was dripping fluid all over the floor, leaving a glistening trail of wet behind me, like a snail. The nurse secured the most comfortable pair of mesh underwear, something Hanes could only dream of duplicating. But, the fluid didn't stop there. After so many hours later, I was delivering a ton of fluid right along with a baby. Where was it coming from? The IV? How much fluid was in that drip bag?

During my second pregnancy I felt what I thought was a kick from the baby that was a little harder than normal. It was immediately followed by the sensation of warmth. One you might only ever experience while sleeping with a full bladder and dreaming of relaxing in a pool of warm water.

This time it was a weak leak. Like I had just run over a tiny nail. Panty liners probably would have been fine, but I had already invested in the pillow size pads that could absorb an entire body of water. So I rolled with it.

I was a week shy of forty weeks, and I had already lost my mucous plug a few times, in little, breakaway gobs. Like unwelcome guests it kept returning. It would leave, I would be excited that the end was near, and then nothing would happen. Then I'd lose it again. This went on for six weeks. By the time my amniotic sac had broken, all that was left in there was a baby and a placenta.

This time, I was less focused on monitoring the progress of my leak during labor because this baby wasn't coming out. I confessed to everyone in the room that I couldn't push anymore. I announced that the baby was just going to have to stay the way she was. Head out and shoulders in.

Suddenly, I heard cheers and looked up to find that one doctor and two nurses had multiplied; at least 10 more people were in the room. When had these people come in? How did I not notice the gathering of nurses who were casually watching my lady parts, as if an episode of Duck Dynasty was being projected down there? These people were wildly cheering for me to keep going. There were chants and I think someone did the wave. It was like I was in the Super Bowl of births, except I played way better than the Broncos did in 2014. The crowd gave me a serious run of motivation. It wasn't much longer until my baby was being held up and my husband and I gasped and said: "Oh my gosh, she's huge!" Then, I asked for a beer, but got a piece of chocolate cake instead.

With the birth of my third baby not so far away, I find myself much more relaxed about the whole going into labor deal. I guess I figure it'll happen when it happens. So, if you live nearby and happen to see a glistening trail of water throughout Target, head out to the parking lot. If you offer me a ride, don't worry about your upholstery; I've got my trash bag.

Christina Antus

Christina is Associate Editor at *Mom Babble*. She's been featured multiple times on *In the Powder Room*, *Mom Babble*, *Pregnancy & Newborn Magazine*, *Scary Mommy*, *The Mid*, and *What the Flicka?* She has also been featured on *The Erma Bombeck Writers' Workshop*, *MSN Living* and in the anthology *Martini's and Motherhood: Tales of Wonder, Woe, and WTF?!* When she's not neglecting laundry, or avoiding the grocery store, she's writing and making mediocre meals for her family. You can find her hiding in the closet, eating candy at ChristinaAntus.net.

The Piercing Incident

 Amy Hunter

I was a wild teenager. Translation: rude, disrespectful asshole. When someone is a rude, disrespectful asshole before they turn eighteen, we say "wild teenager" because we know their brain isn't fully developed, thus giving them a bit of a pass on their terrible actions and attitude. I'm not really sure if I deserve that pass now that I'm almost forty, and I'm quite certain I won't take the same shit I doled out when my own children become "wild teenagers," but you should have seen me back in the day. My level of disrespect could have given punk rock a run for its money.

When I turned eighteen, my mother gave me $80 to buy a new pair of shoes for my birthday. So I did what any anti-authority asshole would have done. I bought a $40 pair of shoes and pocketed the rest for my first piercing. Hey, it was the 90s.

In the 90s, most disrespectful assholes were walking around with a nose ring, or an eyebrow piercing. Those were cool, but I was a real pill. I needed to take it to the next level. You're probably thinking nipple ring—good guess, but no. Think lower. Nope, not belly button. Lower. Yup.

At age eighteen, I decided to pierce my lady-bits. Because you never think about the future when you're eighteen.

For ten years I walked around with a genital piercing. Even when I met the man who would become my husband and the father of my children. Even when I grew up and became less of an asshole. I got married and started a normal life keeping house and working. I was an adult.

I thought about taking the piercing out a couple of times, and I tried. But this was a horseshoe shaped ring with a ball in the middle, forming a complete circle and I eventually discovered I would need a professional piercer with a tool to remove it. Who had time for that? And, not that I had suddenly become modest, but I wasn't about to go into a store and drop trou for a stranger to handle my parts. I was an adult now.

That's when I got pregnant.

I'd had an eight-year relationship with my OB-GYN previously, so she knew about the metal I was packing in my pants. "No big deal," she said. The piercing wasn't in the way of my vaginal opening. "Lots of women with genital piercings deliver without issue." After a pleasurable and complication free pregnancy of forty weeks, she checked me into the hospital for an induction.

We arrived on a Thursday night and I tried to get as comfortable as possible in a strange, sterile place with an extra 60 pounds of pregnancy weight on me. They administered medication to ripen my cervix, gave me medication to sleep, and we began to wait.

I awoke the next morning to a doctor breaking my water. "We'd like to push labor along." Yeah, I'm sure. I sat, wondering if this was all normal. They started Pitocin, gave me an epidural, and I waited some more.

After two days in labor—two freaking days!—I'd dilated 3 centimeters.

What!?

My parents came to visit. They sat with my husband and me while my mom made nervous small talk and my father sang me

Broadway show tunes. That's when all the machines began to beep and ding and the nurses and doctor ran in with an oxygen mask for my face.

The next moments were kind of a blur, they were talking to me but all I heard was, "Baby, distress, lack of oxygen, C-section." I waved them along, "Do whatever you have to do." I was worried. I wanted my baby. Now. Healthy. Mine.

The nurses came back in and said, "Um, (cough) Amy? Um, we have to discuss (cough) your jewelry."

"Jewelry? She's not wearing any jewelry," Mom said.

Oh, shit. After all these years, I'd never told my mom about my eighteenth birthday gift to myself. My husband understood and shooed my parents out the door while I dealt with the nurses. I took the oxygen mask off my face. "What's the problem? I was told this wouldn't be a problem." The nurse with the bigger set of balls started, "Well sugar, it wasn't a problem for natural labor but it's a huge problem for a surgical situation."

The reason you're not allowed to wear jewelry while having a C-section is that, worst case scenario, if they need to bring you back to life with those paddles, well, wherever you have jewelry will get "burned". Lovely.

Another nurse chimed in, "We're gonna have to try and cut it off."

Cut it off? What!?

So there I was, being prepped for C-section, when three nurses came into my room with a fucking bolt cutter.

A big. Ass. Bolt cutter.

And they were going for my vagina with it.

While I'm not an incredibly vain person, all the possible options of what could go wrong were swimming through my head while I clenched my eyes shut and cursed my asshole teenage self for this stupid, careless decision I'd made ten years ago.

It's a really good thing my belly was as massive as it was at the time. I didn't need to see that. It took several attempts to discover that surgical grade steel was not going to give in to the bolt cutter and eventually we made the decision to put tape over the piercing, praying that I wouldn't need to be brought back to life and BBQ my bits.

Thankfully, they didn't have to.

And, compared to the visual of my labia being excised by a bolt cutter, a C-section was less painful than I'd imagined.

My baby was born into this world. Perfect and pink, and all memories of the labor and the complications and the bolt cutter were forgotten.

Then I got pregnant again.

I was almost eight months along when I went for my final monthly visit and my new OB-GYN, a fantastically flaming man with an amazing sense of humor, examined me and said, "Girl! You still haven't had your piercing removed?"

Ugh. I was dreading going to a piercing shop, in all my pregnant glory, to pay someone to examine my nudity and remove this piercing. "You can just tape it again," I attempted. Yeah, that wasn't so bad. "No way, sister," yelled my doctor. "That's not how I do a C-section! That's your homework. Get that thing out."

Shit.

I went to a local piercing and tattoo shop and they had a huge sign of the front door that read, "If you are pregnant, sunburned, drunk, high, broke, or rude, do not enter."

This should be fun. I swallowed my pride, and the last breath of air I could muster as I walked through the door. I waddled inside up to the desk where a girl styled to look like a pin-up chick, waited. Her hair was in a huge curl upon her head, amazing tattoos adorned her slender body. *I'm so out of my league*, I thought.

I explained the situation to her in a nervous, stream-of-consciousness, run-on sentence. I told her about the bolt cutters, and my complete procrastination in getting this odd circumstance taken care of. I told her I'd probably have to deliver this baby myself; squatting in the woods somewhere if I didn't get this piercing removed, as my doctor wanted to wring my neck.

She took me to her little medical-office simulated part of the shop. She had me remove my underwear, lift my dress and sit on a table. She used betadine solution, grabbed a small metal tool and popped the ball from the horseshoe piercing. She removed it, cleaned it and gave it to me in a little plastic bag, remarking on the war wounds the piece now had on it: three large grooves from the bolt cutter incident.

All together I've had three successful C-sections resulting in three beautiful sons.

I carry the piercing in my wallet to remind me of how far I've come from being an asshole. But, like most adults, owning up to my mistakes, and resolving them, also means knowing when to close that chapter entirely. For example, my mom still doesn't know about my "jewelry" and why should I go running to mommy and tell her about it when I'm finally a grown-up mom myself?

Amy Hunter

Amy Hunter grew up in the suburbs of Long Island singing Barbara Streisand hits into her hairbrush. When she's not writing her hilarity-fueled parenting memoir as The Outnumbered Mother, she's a Florida-living, butt-wiping, soccer team–carting, gourmet chef–attempting, tennis skirt–wearing (but non-tennis playing), self-proclaimed, bad mamma jamma to three sons and a very understanding husband. You can find Amy's work as a featured writer for *Scary Mommy* in the parenting anthology *Scary Mommy's Guide to Surviving the Holidays*, and online at *The Huffington Post*, and *In the Powder Room*. Amy blogs at TheOutnumberedMother.com.

Labor, Delivery, and Naked Driving

 Mary Widdicks

Do you know where you were five hours after giving birth to your first child?

For most people the answer is obvious: the hospital. Not true for me.

Exactly five hours after my first son was born I was driving myself home from the hospital, on the wrong side of the road, in a foreign country, without wearing any pants.

Considering the unorthodox ending, my birth story started out surprisingly normal, even textbook, with a few contractions and a shocking amount of fluids.

I'd been laboring gradually and impatiently at home for most of a day when, without warning, the dam broke. My mom and husband were cooking dinner while I bounced uncomfortably on my yoga ball trying to hurry the labor process along when I heard a pop from somewhere inside my body like someone had snapped a rubber band in my belly. This was my first baby, so I'm not sure how I knew what the sound meant, but from some ancient and primitive part of my brain came a sudden impulse to save my carpet.

I jumped up off my ball and had just enough time to yell to my husband to "get a towel," while squeezing my lady bits as tightly as I could with a watermelon bearing down on my hips. Somehow we managed to cover the rug before the worst of the mess hit the floor. This was less due to my superhuman Kegel abilities and more to the fact that my sweat pants had absorbed about a gallon of amniotic fluid and were now sagging like a diaper around my knees.

Good thing I have an extra pair of maternity pants in my hospital bag, I thought to myself before waddling off to clean myself up.

I wish someone had thought to warn me that the initial blast of slimy liquid was just the beginning of the fun I was about to experience. Alas my research, television, and movies had let me down.

I was completely unprepared for the fact that when your water breaks it keeps on flowing until the baby is born.

Assuming the worst of my pants-wetting was behind me, I donned my last pair of sweats, slapped on a menstrual pad, and started panicking about the now inevitable birth that was happening today.

We needed to get to the hospital.

Unfortunately, my son had chosen to arrive a week early and caught us slightly unprepared. My husband and I were living in Lancaster, England, at the time and my mom had flown in from the United States only the day before. We had ambitious plans to teach my mom to drive on the left side of the road and practice navigating the windy route to the hospital several times before I went into labor, but sadly none of it had come to fruition.

I was doubled over in pain and my husband didn't have a valid driver's license, so it was straight into the driving deep-end for Grandma. We loaded up the car with approximately three tons of stuff I was certain I couldn't live without at the hospital, and my mom jumped nervously into the cramped driver's seat of our aptly-named Nissan Micra. I rode in the passenger seat barking instructions about left-hand turns, crossing traffic, and not mowing down pedestrians in zebra crossings.

It was dark, stormy, and terrifying outside. I was gripping the dashboard with white knuckles drunk on a vicious cocktail of fear and pain. I told everyone it was because of the contractions, but honestly, if my pants hadn't already been wet from my water breaking, I probably would have wet them during that drive.

Somehow, we all made it to the hospital alive and without fighting. Despite the fact that the hospital was half a mile from our house, my contractions seemed to have increased in intensity tenfold during the journey. By the time we reached the front desk in the maternity ward, my mind had left my body and been replaced by some sort of primal, lizard-brain–driven, Amazonian woman.

There was another pregnant girl in front of us at reception so we were forced to wait, pacing the hallways for the next mind-numbing contraction to strike. The girl in front of me couldn't have been more than sixteen years old and was literally clutching her teddy bear to her chest. She was explaining calmly and sweetly to the midwife that her contractions were pretty regular at fifteen to twenty minutes apart and were starting to get uncomfortable.

It was around this point in their conversation that I felt the telltale tightening in my stomach signaling I was about to be run down by another freight train contraction. The nurse looked up from her desk just as my legs started to buckle and I had to take a rather ungraceful squat-lean against the wall to keep from toppling over. She waited patiently while I grimaced in pain, rubbing my body up and down on the wall trying to find a way to distract myself from the fact that I was exploding.

Once the contraction passed and I crumpled in a sweaty, breathless heap on the floor, she turned to the young girl, who was looking appropriately terrified, and asked if it would be okay if she checked me in first.

The next few hours went by in a blur of nudity, bodily fluids, searing pain, and very unladylike grunting sounds. The comfy clothes and bathrobes I had packed in my hospital bag sat untouched on top of the MP3 player along with the snacks I was never going to use. Modern conveniences meant nothing to me anymore. I wandered freely around the delivery room, without a stitch of clothing, in what must have looked like some sort of bacchanal ritual complete with squatting, grunting, and howling at the moon.

Less than four hours after my water broke, my firstborn son took his first breaths in this world, in a grand display of goopy, disgusting pyro-technics, as my husband describes the experience. All I remember saying at the time was "Does he have hair?" Clearly I had my priorities in order.

Once my ravaged and war-torn vagina had been sewn up and the pediatrician had checked the baby, I decided I would rest better at home in my own bed. So as soon as I could walk and use the bathroom comfortably, the midwives released me from the maternity ward, a mere five hours after my son was born.

Now that my brain had returned to my body, and the primitive she-creature that had given birth to my first child on hands and knees on a mat in the middle of a concrete floor had vacated, I was suddenly aware of my nudity. I found my shirt right away, but no pants.

Then I saw them, crumpled in a waterlogged heap in the corner where they had been strewn during the chaos of the night.

My one and only pair of maternity sweats were completely soaked through with cold, leftover amniotic fluid.

Not a problem, I thought to myself, *I'll just borrow some scrubs.*

Except, another fun fact that my pregnant predecessors forgot to mention to me was that you still look about seven months pregnant even after delivering your baby. Even the largest pair of scrubs in the maternity ward was way too small to fit over my swollen abdomen.

The way I saw it, I had two choices: I could wait in the hospital while my husband walked to town to buy me a pair of pants or I could wrap a towel around my waist and call it a day. I chose the latter.

I also chose, in the interest of my child's safety and my mental health, to drive myself home while my mom sat safely in the passenger seat. So there I was, five hours post-delivery, driving along the narrow English roads, boobs leaking colostrum, my vagina still numb from the stitches, wearing extremely fashionable mesh underwear provided to me by the hospital, nothing but a towel draped around my legs, and a stupid grin plastered to my face.

I must have looked like a deranged mental patient to my fellow drivers, but to me my birth story was the most beautiful, natural, and completely disgusting experience of my life.

I wouldn't change a thing.

Mary Widdicks

Mary Widdicks is a mom to two boys and one girl. Being outnumbered in the family means that sometimes her voice gets drowned out by fart jokes and belching contests. She started OutmannedMommy.com so she'd have a place to escape the testosterone and share her hilarious life with the rest of the world. Mary's writing has been featured on parenting sites such as *Mamapedia, Mamalode, In the Powder Room, Pregnant Chicken,* and *Scary Mommy.* She is a regular contributor on *BLUNTmoms* and has been honored as a 2014 Voice of the Year by BlogHer, and Badass Blogger of the Year for 2014 by The Indie Chicks.

That's Not Sweat

 Jessica Azar

As I waddled into the hospital elevator, I contemplated how different this delivery scenario was from the births of my first two children. My oldest's birth was a scary, stressful one that ended with him staying in the NICU for a week, and I was terrified that my second son's birth would end the same way, so I had been anxious during his delivery. The atmosphere and my mood this time were more relaxed; I had been through this rodeo two other times in the past three years and knew what I was doing. As the elevator dinged and opened, I stepped onto the labor and delivery floor and marveled at the calming quiet of the ward. It contrasted sharply with the din of my chaotic household, where my mother was currently watching my boys. Several years prior I wouldn't have thought of a hospital visit to give birth as a vacation, but I was practically giddy at the thought of being waited on hand and foot for three days, all while I would be getting to enjoy the newborn scent of my little one. Not exactly a Jamaican beach, but to an overwrought mom, it sounded like bliss. We were finally there! The big day that I would bring more estrogen into our male-dominated household.

I strolled into my assigned delivery suite, casually returning the waves and smiles from nurses I'd met before: a warm welcome for a labor and delivery frequent flyer. After that day's nurse gave me the standard undressing and urine sample instructions, she left me to it. My husband came in the room while I was undressing and made suggestive gestures while grinning at me, proposing we test out the hospital bed and said, "We could try to get her out the fun way..."

I laughed and joked. "Um, no, that's what got us here and our efforts to evict her before now haven't worked. I'm sticking with the medical route today." He smiled and settled down in the room's recliner, dressed in a pink polo shirt he'd chosen to celebrate our daughter's birth, resigned to his position on the proverbial bench for today's main event.

It was such a relief to finally be there, knowing that my baby would be born that very day. I had been telling the doctor for three weeks that she was trying to make her entrance into the world. My baby girl had sent me to labor and delivery multiple times after my thirty-sixth week of pregnancy, only to have my labor stopped by various medicines. She was doing her best to get out, but nobody would put me out of my bloated, whale-like misery.

Keeping up with the demands, both physically and mentally, of my almost three- and almost two-year-old sons, was getting harder by the day. After a sonogram the prior week indicated that she was already 8 pounds and 7 ounces, I begged to be induced, as I was terrified of a C-section and I was scared that a baby bigger than my son's 8 pound 9 ounce birth would tear me in two. Even though I explained that another week baking in my Applebee's Boneless Buffalo Wings-infused uterus would lead to a gargantuan newborn, my doctor ignored my totally logical case for induction. Finally, the doctor had scheduled a formal labor induction at the thirty-nine-week mark, and all it took was a tiny bit of Pitocin to throw those contractions into full gear. My labor progressed rapidly until my doctor commented that my daughter had not traveled any lower into the carefree highway of my birth canal. After checking her position he realized that she was, in fact, stuck.

Stuck.

I was scared, confused, and pissed off. This little girl had been trying to make her way into the world and abandon the studio apartment of my uterus that was growing smaller by the day, only to be stopped at every turn. Her escape efforts thwarted, she had no other option but to stay put, and now it seemed that she would stay, indefinitely.

Mildly amused at the irony, but horrified at the implications, I asked, "Well what do we do now? How will you get her out!?" My doctor had legendary experience with high-risk births and complicated deliveries, so my confidence in him was high, but I knew this would not be an easy ordeal. My doctor snapped a latex glove on one of his hands and looked at me seriously, saying "Jessica, I'm going to try to flip her to the way she should be facing for delivery, and dislodge her from the space she's wedged herself into. If that doesn't work, we will have to do an emergency C-section."

A sensation of dread washed over me as a killer contraction seared through my body. I was furious! If they had only listened to me, this might have been avoided, but I didn't have long to dwell on that thought. My doctor said, "I'm going in" and inserted both hands into my neither regions in an attempt to help my angel do a backflip. It hurt like hell, and after three attempts to move her during a series of contractions, he stopped, wiped his sweating brow on his sleeve and told my nurse, "Go get the attending on this floor. I'm going to need backup."

What in the fresh hell did that mean!? This was not a hostage situation where he needed to be covered, and I had honestly never heard of doctors delivering in tandem. Was he going to hold onto my doctor's waist and help him pull the baby out of me? I snorted at the thought of a loud "pop" noise, like a cork shooting from a bottle of champagne, as my daughter came into the world, but that thought vanished when the older doctor walked into the room. My doctor briefed him on the situation in hushed tones as a couple of extra nurses quietly slipped into the room. I assessed the growing audience in my delivery room as both doctors monitored the timing of contractions, and then both went in for the kill.

Before I knew it they were both elbows deep in my lady parts, attempting to force her into the correct position. Seeing this, I thought, "My God. I look like a car having its oil changed and spark plugs replaced." My husband stared with wide eyes at the two men rearranging my insides, probably wondering if we would ever be able to have marital relations again. About that time, a group of nurses gang-tackled my huge belly in an attempt to aid the doctors in moving the baby to her rightful place. I felt like the air had been knocked from my body as they attacked me, but internally I felt the baby shift greatly.

The doctors cheered at their success and the nurses placed my arms on the bed rails and yelled at me to "Puuush!!" which, even though I was exhausted, I happily attempted. In focusing my energy and strength on the pushing, I closed my eyes. After opening them, I saw my doctor squinting his eyes closed tightly as he demanded that someone give him a towel. I thought to myself, "Wow, he's going the distance. I owe him a drink after this." They instructed me to push again, and my little girl, with a thick, full head of black hair popped out. No "pop" sound accompanied her womb exit, but I didn't care. We had both made it out of this craziness alive.

The doctor, looking at her as he pulled her free, said, "Easily a 10-pound baby. Wow. That's a healthy little girl, right there!"

Thoughts of "I freaking told you so!" sounded off in my head, but I was drained of all energy and happy to be done with the worst of the delivery. Our daughter, Mary Ellen, was weighed, measured, and had her footprints taken by the nurses before being swaddled and handed to me. According to their calculations, she was 9 pounds, 10 ounces and 23 inches of beautiful baby girl, and she was mine.

I tenderly kissed her little face and my husband leaned over us to kiss us both. He smiled at me and said, "You do know that you peed in the doctor's face when you pushed, right?" Stunned, I said, "I did? When!?" and then it clicked in my head. He wasn't wiping away sweat with that towel; I had given him the fire hydrant treatment. Too exhausted and robbed of modesty to be overly embarrassed, I waved the thoughts away like rogue flies, snuggled the baby, and demanded a Coke classic. I was determined to enjoy my "vacation" before reentering the world as a mommy to three kids under age three. Also, I needed to ask the nurse if it should feel like my insides were about to fall out of my baby chute.

No matter how many times you've been through a given situation, know that you're never truly prepared for all scenarios. That goes double for anything to do with pregnancy or parenting. All you can do is weather the storm, enjoy the sweet moments, and try not to a piss a stream in your doctor's face. But if you do, know that he's probably endured worse. At least that's what mine told me when I apologized and thanked him for bringing my daughter safely into the world.

Jessica Azar

Jessica Azar writes while raising four stair-step kids, known affectionately as The Herd, with her husband and college sweetheart in her Alabama hometown. She blogs at Herd-Management.com and humorously details the adventures and mishaps of being a homeschooling, work-at-home-mom. She also happens to like running and single malt scotch a whole lot. Jessica co-edited a mental health anthology entitled *Surviving Mental Illness Through Humor*, and has had essays published in humor anthologies, including *Clash of the Couples*. She is a *Huffington Post* Blogger, *POPSUGAR Select* Blogger, a *NickMom* Ambassador/Writer, and does marketing work for various prominent brands. Her published work can be read on *POPSUGAR*, *Huffington Post*, *Scary Mommy*, *NickMom.com*, *Venn Magazine*, *BLUNTmoms* and other online locations.

Beware the Advice Brigade!

 Melissa Charles

No matter if it's your first baby, or your sixth, somehow you become the target for unsolicited advice and comments. Unless you tell nobody that you're expecting, or hole up in your house until after baby's eighteenth birthday, it's going to happen.

I've found that the Advice Brigade tends to fall into particular categories:

The Pregnancy Posse: These are the folks that hover around your belly, barking orders and instructions about what you should/shouldn't eat, do, buy, think, or feel. They all have horror stories of folks who did the opposite of what they're ordering, with dire consequences. "You shouldn't eat fish! My cousin's step-sister's brother-in-law's wife's best friend ate fish, and her baby? Performs at Sea World now. You don't want your baby performing with seals, do you?!"

Reality: Following a healthy diet and the appropriate restrictions as set out by your medical professional is reasonable. Folks that lose their ever-loving minds over your diet need a hobby.

The Birth Brigade: Similar to the Pregnancy Posse, in fact, they can be in both groups, and often are. They're obsessed with the birth process. They'll tell you that you can't have meds and recite scary anecdotes about women who have. "Susie had drugs during labor. Her little Tommy is eight and he's still stoned from that!" Or, conversely, there are those who will mock your plans for an un-medicated birth. "Yeah, right. You'll be begging for an epidural! I know a woman who tried to do the all-natural thing, and her head exploded, right there in the delivery room!"

Reality: Your body, your birth, your choices. Unless there is a medical reason for it to be otherwise (e.g. C-section), you are the one in charge of your labor and delivery. There is no failure when it comes to how any woman manages her labor.

Natural Nancies and the Medical Marys. These folks are a subset of the Birth Brigade. The groups are completely opposed to the other. The first believes that all women are best served out of the hospital, that pregnancy needs no medical intervention, ever, and that if you were a real woman, you could give birth on your own. In a forest. With only woodland creatures as attendants. The second believes that anyone who doesn't have her baby in a hospital should be arrested, shackled to a gurney, and forced into a fully medicated birth.

Reality: Again, your body, your birth, your choice. Be it a home birth, or a hospital one, a safe delivery of the baby is what truly matters. Mom being as comfortable and confident as possible has been shown to be a positive aspect of managing labor.

Gender Groupies: "Every man needs a son!" "Every woman has to have a daughter!" They will also lose their minds if you refuse to find out the baby's gender before birth, or refuse to share it with everyone who asks. These are also the folks that will demand you try again if you don't have one of each gender. "After this one is born, you have to try for a boy/girl! If you don't have a boy/girl, you'll end up living under a rock from depression, and never know the pure magic and bliss that comes with having a son/daughter!" Or, "You poor woman. All those boys!" Or, "Your poor husband. How will he cope with a houseful of women?"

Reality: Other folk's gender bias isn't your problem. Enjoy the kids you have.

Size Snipers: It doesn't matter if you choose to have one child or a dozen, Size Snipers will explain why you're terribly, horribly wrong, and explain the psychological damage you're inflicting upon your child. "Only children are lonely! Only children are selfish! Only children can't cope with the real world!" "You're just being selfish, having that many children!" "You can't do for all those kids!" "Don't you know what causes that yet?" "Can't you manage birth control?"

Reality: Some folks are going to have something snarky to say if you have anything but the boy and girl set that they've deemed acceptable. Unless they're financially supporting your family, it's none of their business. Your family size is nobody else's business.

Age Angsters: "You're too young to have a baby!" "You're too old to have a baby!"

Reality: As far as I can figure out, the only right age to have a baby for some folks is a week between your twenty-sixth and twenty-seventh birthday. Maybe. Otherwise, you're wrong.

Naming Naggers: They have a list of acceptable names for you to use, none of which includes the names you've already picked out, and almost always includes their name, or a variation of it. "But, Great-Great-Great Uncle Dishwater Scuzzy Suds needs a name sake! He'll haunt you if you don't name your baby after him!" "I knew a girl named that. She travels with the sideshow, biting the heads off of newborn puppies! You don't want your daughter biting the heads off of newborn puppies, do you!?" "You can't name him that! Four hundred years ago, someone with that name insulted our ancestor! It would be saying you hate this family if you use that name!" "Matilda is so a boy name! I read about a famous movie star naming her son that!"

Reality: Your baby, your choice. Often, the folks that yell the loudest about family tradition/honoring family members have already had children. They had their chance to honor Great Uncle Festeritis … and didn't. Also, remember that sooner or later, your child will want to know why the heck you named him "Clem Kadiddle Hopper," if you give in to pressure from that name's supporters. (Personally, I always put Supreme Court Justice in front of any names we're considering. If it sounds good with that, we're golden.)

Spectator Sport: These are the folks that believe that birth is something best shared. Preferably in a stadium, with every last detail being broadcast on the big screen. God forbid you don't invite all the grandparents, great-grandparents, uncles, aunts, cousins, neighbors, the mailman, and the dog catcher to witness the miracle of birth. It's flat out selfish, you know, to only have you, your spouse, and whatever medically necessary people there. You'd think that it's all about you, that it's your body or something. Ha!

Reality: Your birth, your rules. You want a crowd of folks in there? Have at it! You want it just to be you and your husband? Then that's how it needs to be. Many hospitals do have a way to register privately, if you have any concerns about your desire to not have a cheerleading squad present.

Feeding Frenzy: These are the ones who insist that there is only one right way to feed a baby, and to not do as they insist is to doom your child for life. "I know someone that breastfed their baby, and he's twenty-two now, and still coming home to nurse!" "Breastfed babies are spoiled! They never get off the boob and can't socialize with anyone else!" "Formula feeding is neglectful! Any mother that truly loves her baby will nurse." "If you won't breastfeed your baby, he's going to be stupid!"

Reality: As long as baby is being fed, is growing and thriving, is being held, nurtured and loved, it's okay. For a myriad of reasons, some women are unable to nurse, or unable to nurse for as long as they'd hoped. Please take comfort that nursing isn't the be all and end all of your motherhood. As long as you are taking care of your baby, you're rocking this Momma gig. Honest. I also promise that, breast or bottle, Junior will be off both before prom.

Ⓐ Ⓑ Ⓒ

Above all else, remember this: your choices for your birth and your child are just that. Yours.

Perfectly acceptable responses to any and all of the above might include: "We'll give that all the consideration it deserves." "We've got it covered." "We've made our decision, thank you."

Slightly stronger responses might include: "We'll do what's best for our baby." "I already have a medical professional involved." "We're comfortable and confident in our decisions, thank you."

Blunt responses, for those that just won't stop: "No." "It's none of your business." "Asked and answered. It's not open for discussion." "Your approval is neither required nor desired."

And remember that old saying, "Opinions are like butts. Everyone has one." In the case of pregnancy, labor and delivery, it's your butt on the line, so it's your opinion that counts.

Melissa Charles

Melissa "The Imp" Charles spends her days being The Wife to Wolf and Mom to Five Minions at home, ranging in age from sixteen years to eighteen months. Between homeschooling, blogging, and general all around chaos, she spends her days like a demented pinball, spinning from one thing to the next. You can find her blogging at NotAStepfordLife.com.

This Ain't Your Mama's Birth

 Lisa René LeClair

Ah, pregnancy: A time of self-loathing, elephantine movement and the inability to go more than thirty seconds without needing to pee. Scratch that. Make it twenty seconds.

Working out had always been a part of my daily routine and something I wasn't willing to give up easily because of an undisciplined embryo that would rather sleep in. So, each morning, I would waddle through the front door of the gym, proud and defiant, oblivious to the giggles and whispers circling around my ill-fitting spandex. I'd wriggle my way past the twenty-somethings, careful not to release a gust of maternity gas, and find a dark corner all to myself. And it was there that I had the courage to complete a series of half-assed sit-ups in front of my only true friend: a tearful reflection of myself.

The doctor described labor pain as a muscle spasm in your abdomen that would last anywhere from sixty to ninety seconds. "Anything less," I thought, "will be ignored." So, it was no surprise that I showed up at the gym on the day that I went into labor, oscillating like a rotisserie chicken on an elliptical machine going nowhere. I went home that morning feeling dejected, crushed, and severely constipated, followed by burning waves of discomfort and a dull pain on my lower right side. Still, I wrote it off as heartburn, got myself dressed, and called the doctor, expecting little.

"How far apart are the contractions?"

"I don't even know if they are contractions," I cried. "It just feels like I have to go to the bathroom, and I've already squeezed out an entire middle-class family!"

We agreed that I would go to the hospital just as soon as my mother arrived; she was flying in from Atlanta that day. We further agreed that my husband would be the one to pick her up, which sparked my second call.

"Hey. I just got off the phone with the doctor and she wants me to swing by the hospital. Would you mind picking up mom at the airport?"

"What's going on? Are you in labor?"

"No," I reassured him, "She just wants to have a look."

"Okay. What do you want me to tell your mom?"

"Nothing! Just tell her I wasn't feeling good. I'll go ahead and pack a bag so I'm ready when you get here."

"Pack a bag? I thought you said it wasn't labor!"

"I don't know what it is, but I'm taking my stuff just in case." My mother's flight was due in around 11:00 am. By 12:55 pm, I was pacing the floors.

My phone rang.

"Hi, mom."

"What's going on? Are you in labor?"

"No! The doctor just wants to make sure everything is okay. What time are you guys going to be here?"

"Well, your husband missed the exit to the airport and had to circle around a few times, but we should be there in about twenty minutes."

By the time they pulled up, I was standing in the driveway with a miserable disposition and an overnight bag full of tears.

"I knew it! You're in labor!" shrieked my mother as she sprang from the car to greet me.

My husband, who was fumbling to stuff me into the backseat and pestering me with questions and nervous energy, was a wreck. And just as he reached around to grab the buckle, another wave of pain swooped down and punched my inner core, forcing out two-and-a-half-hours of repressed anger.

"Can you please just get in the f—ing car and drive!?"

The nurses on staff were all smiles and as eager to please as bellhops at the Ritz —until *she* came in.

The doctor was all business at first, glancing at charts, poking monitors, and asking all the right questions. And then she chuckled as if she had just heard a bad joke.

"What? Is everything okay?"

"Everything is fine," she replied, "But you're only half a centimeter dilated."

"What does that mean? You're not going to send me home, are you?"

"I'd like you to walk around for a little while and see if that speeds things up. I'll see you back here in an hour."

With that, she sent me on my way, down a cold, marble hallway, to waddle in self-pity and pray that I'd win that epidural grand prize. And, though I felt like a dead man walking and was certain I'd be spending the next twenty-four hours in the lobby, it appeared that my dramatic pleas for mercy had finally paid off.

"Well..." began the doctor, "it looks like you're up to one centimeter now."

"ONE?!" I cried, unaware of any real tears, "Are you kidding?"

The doctor, feeling particularly sorry for me, told me to relax while she placed a call to my OB-GYN. Then she stepped away from my semi-private *sheet curtain* and began to dial the phone. But sheet curtains aren't soundproof and I could hear everything she was saying, even the part where she laughed at my cervical dilatation.

"Shit," I mouthed to my pillars of non-strength, "they're going to send me home!"

But a few minutes later, the doctor rounded the corner with the best news we had heard all day. Not only would I be spending the night at *Chateau Bayfront*, I had beaten the odds and won the Holy Grail of Anesthesiology: the paralyzing epidural sweepstakes.

Once the epidural kicked in, nothing seemed to bother me. I didn't even mind that my last meal was the glass of orange juice I had thrown up the night before. But the itching was out of control and, apparently, my crackhead impersonation had caught the attention of one of the nurses.

"Oh," she grinned, "That's one of the side effects of the epidural. If you'd like, I can give you some Benadryl."

"Thank you." I beamed as the itching subsided, "This is *AMAZING!*"

But an hour later, she was back to inform me that the Benadryl had inadvertently put the baby to sleep. "It's nothing to worry about," she assured, "we're just going to give you a little oxygen to get the baby moving again."

As they secured a mask over my face, I saw my mother run out of the room in a paranoid frenzy with my husband trailing behind. It wasn't until the next day that I found out what he had said to get her back into the room: "Put your game face on, Arlene, and get back in there. You're scaring my wife!"

A few hours later, I felt a tiny snap down in my lady parts.

"Mom? I think my water just broke!"

Despite having had three children of her own, my mother had never actually witnessed childbirth. According to her, in those days women were knocked out until after the baby was born, leaving no visible trace of the wreckage left behind by a surge of crashing water. Her only acknowledgment came in the form of a repulsed commentary coming from between my legs:

"Oh my God. That is disgusting! I thought it was just supposed to be water!?"

Around 10:30 pm, the doctor came in with a patronizing smile and a prescription for a good night's sleep. "It's not going to happen tonight," she laughed. "See you in the morning!"

While everyone else slept soundly amid the flickering monitor lights, I lay motionless on a three-inch mattress, folded up like a king-size taco.

That's when it happened. I pressed the call button and waited for what seemed like an eternity.

"Yes?" cooed the nurse as she tiptoed into the room.

"I felt something—down there!"

"Well," she began in an uncertain tone, "let's just have a look then, shall we?"

It was obvious, by the way that her laughter ceased, that something was amiss.

"What is it?"

"I can't believe it. You're ten centimeters!"

So there I was, spread eagle on a mattress with the husband holding one leg and my mom holding the other. Just as I began pushing my way to freedom, my mother announced to the world that she doesn't think she can go through with it.

"Go through with what?" I shrieked, with tears pouring out. "Mom? Where are you going? Wait! Don't drop my leg!"

Several minutes, and many contractions later, we heard the bathroom door open and the sound of a familiar voice coughing.

"I'm okay," my mother assured us, "Let's do this!"

And do it we did.

My daughter is now almost eight. She is smart, beautiful and hilarious beyond words. Still, I often wonder what life would have been like had I opted to waive my rite of passage, that long, winding and excruciating route to motherhood. But after a million cherished moments, warm hugs and relentless giggles, it has occurred to me that the worst ten months of my life were actually the best I ever had. And I would gladly do it all over again.

Remember, it may be ten months, but it's worth every second for a lifetime of love!

Lisa René LeClair

From party girl to corporate slug turned entrepreneur/ business owner, she thought she had seen it all—until she got pregnant! Lisa René LeClair (aka, Sassypiehole) is a writer, humorist, social media junkie and, most importantly, a mother. When she's not giggling with her pint-sized protégé or pretending to sign autographs in front of a bathroom mirror, you can find Lisa sitting at her desk working on her blog, Sassypiehole.com, wearing coffee stained pajamas and a shit-eating grin, living the dream.

Do Not Touch A Pregnant Woman's Belly Without Asking

 Sarah Cottrell

There is a dirty secret about being pregnant that people don't seem to share with a first-time mom-to-be: She will become public property. Everything about her pregnancy will be questioned, commented on, and even her body will be touched, poked, patted, and rubbed by anyone and everyone, even strangers.

When I was pregnant with my first child, I was enamored with every single part of it. Aches and pains, bloating and glowing, growing and expanding, it didn't matter because I felt that I was embarking on a rite of passage from womanhood into motherhood and I was Carpe Diem-ing the hell out of it.

It wasn't long before my innie became an outie and I was waddling my way through my days. As I was inching ever closer to my due date I was bursting through my maternity clothes; almost weekly I needed to swing by the local department store to pick up a new maternity bra or stretchy pants. One could say that I was becoming something of a fixture at that place.

On one particularly adventurous afternoon I found myself browsing the women's apparel section. I had high hopes of finding a knit cardigan that might cover my stained maternity t-shirts. It is astounding how clumsy pregnancy can make a woman. I had a pile of sweaters in my cart and as I was reaching for an oversized knit pullover in a funny shade of ecru, I heard a lady exclaim, "Oh, my! You are huge! You must be carrying twins!"

Let me just say that there are few things more irritating to hear than having your pregnant girth commented on by a complete stranger. *Why yes, you idiot, I am huge, I'm carrying a human being inside me.* My thought bubbles started filling with snarky responses, but my mouth said, "Oh, ha ha! I guess I am really big, but I'm only expecting one."

I pushed my cart on to the next aisle.

While I was trying to mentally calculate just how expensive this trip for stretchy pants was going to be, the lady from the sweater aisle had found her way next to me again.

This woman appeared to be in her 80s. She had a purplish tint to her short, permed gray hair. She wore khakis with brightly colored Crocs poking out from the hem of her creased pants. My eyes wanted to bleed from the garish assault of bright red and green that seemed to glow with their clashing pattern on her holiday-themed turtleneck. In this woman's cart was an oversized beige coat and a leather pocketbook that looked to be about 600 years old.

She smelled like mothballs.

"I don't see a ring on your finger, dear. Are you being taken care of? Oh, honey, I'm sorry, I don't mean to pry. You don't look like one of those girls. Maybe you're retaining water, sweetie, but either way you really ought to have a ring on that finger!"

What the fuck? Seriously? Who is this broad!?

"Oh, gosh. I appreciate your concern, but I'm doing very well."

And with that I smiled and pushed my cart toward the next aisle where I pulled out my cell phone.

Since I just wanted to be alone and was getting pretty damn grouchy, what with the nosy old lady following me around the store, I pretended to make a phone call.

I put the phone to my ear and mouthed a few whispery words. I saw the lady approaching me again but this time I turned my back to her and started walking toward the housewares section. I gestured a few times to really play up the faux phone call.

But, I could smell her coming toward me again. Not only does pregnancy give a woman super hero sniffing powers, but also mothballs carry a lethal dose of potent stink that anyone would find hard to ignore. I ducked behind a display of touristy Maine Coast magnets on a six-foot tall sheet of metal. I felt a bit like a moose trying to hide behind a tree. Surely, if I can't see her then she can't see me, right?

Wrong.

My girth gave me away. That old bitch was coming toward me and there was no place for me to go because I was blocked by the wall of magnets and now a cart filled with cardboard boxes that an employee had just parked in the middle of the aisle while he tried to figure out what he was doing.

If that was not uncomfortable enough then my sudden and desperate urge to pee made it feel just that much more unbearable.

As Mothballs approached me, I felt panic set in. I was trapped. What other inappropriate comment did this lady need to make? Would she begin giving me some crap parenting advice along the lines of "sleep when the baby sleeps"? I didn't know. But my hackles went up and I was ready to burst into tears. Or pee my pants. I wasn't really sure.

Mothballs parked her cart and slowly shuffled over to the pubescent stock boy and said, "Now, listen here young man, you ought to pay more attention to where you put your piles of nonsense! This young lady is with child for goodness sakes!"

My eyebrows went up in surprise. Mothballs was helping me out! My hackles were going down.

She continued, "You move that cart out of the way this instant! Show some respect young man!" The kid looked a little scared, and, frankly, the tone of her voice compelled me to want to stand at attention and smooth out my ketchup-stained shirt. Should I have placed a book on my head and began reciting something!? I had no idea what to do.

The kid fumbled while he piled his boxes back into his cart and moved farther down the aisle. Now that I was free to move I was sure that I would pee my pants. I was squirming a little bit. I pushed my cart toward the center of the aisle in hopes of making a clean get away toward the bathroom, but Mothballs wasn't done with me yet.

"Are you sure you aren't carrying twins? Hahaha. My goodness you are wide, honey! I carried much higher and tighter."

She then reached out and touched my belly.

What. The. Hell?

At this point I was ready to explode. Not only was I about to pee my pants, but Mothballs had me so upset that no amount of diplomacy was going to rein in the crazy surge of hormones that was rushing to be unleashed.

"Hey! Do you mind? I did not invite you to touch my body! For the love of God, lady! I am not carrying twins! Would you kindly keep your damn opinions to yourself!?"

I stood there panting. My pants were a little wet. It was not my finest moment.

"Jesus, calm down. You had ketchup on your shirt and I was trying to wipe it off. No lady in your condition should have to deal with people staring. I didn't want to embarrass you by pointing it out."

She shuffled her cart away.

I burst into tears and waddled to the bathroom where I could clean off the ketchup and deal with the fact that I had just screamed at a perfectly nice old lady and had indeed peed my pants a little bit.

Sarah Cottrell

Sarah lives in Maine with her boat-builder husband and two loud boys. In 2012 she earned her MFA and since then she has been featured on several popular parenting sites including *BlogHer, In The Powder Room, Mamalode*, and she is a regular contributor to *Scary Mommy* and *The Huffington Post*. You can follow the fun on her blog HousewifePlus.BangorDailyNews.com.

Sometimes They Birth Themselves

 Sharon Buckley

As I neared the end of my third pregnancy, rather than feeling more confident than ever about the impending birth, I actually felt less. Plagued as I was by the constant griping of my irritable uterus in the form of frequent contractions, my main concern became the possibility that early labor would come upon me without my ever realizing it. I knew this scenario to be one of legitimate concern given that my second child was born in less than two hours from the time that active labor began, and my only clue of the preceding, early labor stage was when the doctor told me I was six centimeters dilated at a scheduled OB appointment.

Because of the lightning-fast arrival of my second kid, I found myself with what doctors call "precipitous birth," paired with another lovely term that I picked up during my pregnancy, "prodromal labor." During his gestation, I experienced both the best and worst of what labor had to offer in the form of a long, slow (we are talking weeks-long) progression towards early labor, followed by a very quick finish. Whenever someone would express disbelief at the speed of my second delivery, my husband would respond, "Really, she was in labor for almost two months."

My third pregnancy was following much the same pattern; right down to an overnight hospitalization a few weeks shy of the delivery. I needed monitoring until we could be sure that nothing was actually going to come of all the activity taking place in my overactive womb. However, unlike with my second pregnancy, I ultimately found myself pregnant well past the thirty-eight-week, and indeed, even the thirty-nine-week mark.

As the fifth day of the thirty-ninth week dawned, I tried to console myself once again with the thought that, at worst, it would all be over by the weekend. I had caved to my nervous doctor's wishes and scheduled an induction for the coming Saturday in the hopes that seeing a definite endpoint would choke back some of the stress I was feeling about all the rest of the unknown. As worried as I was, however, I did not do more than take quiet note of the regularity of the contractions that made their too-familiar appearance all morning long. Every six to eight minutes they would come, just barely strong enough to notice, but never closer nor stronger, just more regular.

Three hours into this pattern, my husband offered to take my oldest to the store for a quick grocery run while my younger son was napping. I had an impulse to mention my observations, but quelled it. It seems a ridiculous decision now, but at the time I felt any small step towards mobilization would only falsely feed my hopes; I feared the crushing disappointment that would come when they were not realized. After all, those pesky contractions weren't getting any stronger or closer together, and that would be my first sign that this was the real deal, right?

I was also still feeling some pretty fresh guilt over all of the disruption that my hospitalization had caused one month before. It only got more complicated, after all, as the kids added up. It was no longer as simple as dropping everything to rush out to the hospital. Care had to be arranged, and youngsters needed tending to, up until the moment that care arrived. My son was no exception. He made sure to wake from his nap about fifteen minutes after my husband and oldest exited the premises, and five minutes after I decided to lie down.

I walked my tired, achy person-and-a-half up a flight of stairs and back down again to fetch him, and it was after I had clicked the lock on his highchair tray that I felt that first "real" contraction hit. Of course, in my state of denial, I didn't believe it, not right away. I had experienced one or two random doozies before. *One more*, I promised myself. *Then I'll start making some calls.*

As it turned out, it took two more to really convince me, and my mother, who I called first, did not pick up the phone. By the time I started making panicked follow-up calls to my father and husband, I could hardly talk through the fear and pain. Bereft of any further plan, and desperate to find a way to manage increasing levels of pain on my own, I made my way to the floor of the dining room, right beneath the feet of my happily-snacking son. My husband found me there, sprawled out on all fours and wailing like an animal as he rushed through the door with groceries and our daughter in-hand. Fifteen minutes had passed and I was back in the territory of wicked fast precipitous birth.

I was in some sort of primal zone by then—howling, grunting, and making sounds I'd never before made. Husband was in a zone of his own, rushing back and forth between me and the children to grab a pillow here, offer a snack there. Young as he was, my son seemed to sense that something was amiss, while my daughter was far more interested in the fact that her brother had a graham cracker when she had been offered a serving of Corn Chex, instead.

As my husband tried to form a plan (should we pack the kids in the car or wait on my mother?), and keep everyone happy in the meantime, I had one focus in mind: to get myself into the shower. Though it had always been a desire of mine to arrive at the hospital as fresh and clean as possible (God forbid I give birth with spit-up in my hair), to this day I am still not sure if my sudden obsession with it was borne of some instinctual need to delay as my time drew near, or some irrational response to the pain and stress that I was under. Likely, it was some combination of both.

Regardless, my husband was powerless to stop me. I pulled myself forward on hands and knees, long hair dragging along the floor in front of me like a caricature of *The Ring*'s creepy horror show. Instead, he clamored to my cause, quickly cleaning out the tub so that I could sit at the bottom and wash with the removable nozzle. We worked swiftly and efficiently, and when the bath ended, there was nothing for it but to make our way to the car, but I still couldn't see my way to it.

I could hardly lift my leg over the side of the tub. There was so much pressure. Why was there so much pressure? As I made my first attempt, I felt a trickle of fluid. "I think my water is breaking," I choked out. Despite the circumstances, I didn't quite believe it; my husband didn't believe it either. There was no denying the ensuing gush, however, which I dropped my underwear into, sending my husband scrambling for a second pair.

When he returned, I was crouching there, still behind the un-crossable barrier of the tub wall, eyes wide and mouth agape. "I think I feel the head" was all I could manage to croak out before sliding to a sitting position and screaming more loudly than I had ever had the courage to scream before. I watched all semblance of control flee before me in the shape of a tiny protruding head. Somewhere in the distance my husband was asking if he should call 9-1-1, and I was nodding, and he was losing the call and trying again, but for me there was only the moment and the inevitable.

I was powerless to stop as it pushed its way out, slowly but surely, and the scream continued to push its way out, too, from as much a place of fear as a place of pain. As ready as I thought I had been, I wasn't ready, not for this, not this way. Then it had happened; the head was out. The little eyes were blinking in the blinding whiteness, and I was trying to figure out what it was that I was supposed to be doing.

Somewhere in the back of my mind the memories of previous births were returning, and the voices that narrated them. "Push with the contractions," they said. But those horrible, enveloping pains were over and done with, the worst was behind me, and the baby was right there, ready to come the rest of the way.

I was oblivious to my husband fiddling with the phone beside me; I gave a hesitant push. Nothing. I waited a beat, for a feeling, a sign. It was the baby who gave me one. With no doctor or nurse around to do the job, those tiny little shoulders started turning themselves, rotating to find the ideal position for passage through the canal. I nearly cried in shock, awe, and sheer pride, but first I did what instinct told me to do and pushed again. Thankfully, distracted as he was, my husband still had eyes on us and dove right in to make the catch, just as the 9-1-1 operator finally connected.

"Mywifejsuthadababyinthebathtubwe'reat123MainStreet!" he managed to yelp, as he caught and cradled his newborn. Next he tried to provide an answer to the mystery we'd waited nine long months to solve. "It's a boy—no, it's a girl!" he cried, but the only answer I needed to hear was the soft wailing of my brand-new baby as she was laid on my chest, by none other than her father. Not one to be intimidated by the many roles he had to play that day, he was also the bearer of the happy news to the siblings standing by in the next room, but truth be told they were more interested in the snacks before them than the new playmate around the corner.

We were the talk of the hospital when the ambulance finally delivered us there. News of the "Bathtub Baby" spread from nurse to nurse, and shift to shift. *Born in just under an hour with only her father present at the birth and her older siblings in the next room the whole time!* But the version I best remember was the one I told to the pediatrician who examined her during our stay. "She basically birthed herself," I joked to him.

"Well, maybe she'll become an obstetrician," he said with a smile.

Maybe she will. And she'll be able to boast her first delivery as her own.

Sharon Buckley

Sharon J. Buckley is a stay-at-home mom with three kids four-and-under. While she was once known for her pretty voice and a penchant for the arts, she now spends much of her time trying to stay sane via social media and moonlighting as a blogger when the rare opportunity arises. Though she sticks mainly to her own blog, www.FindingVanillaOctopus.com, she has been featured as a guest-writer for various other blogs as well. She hopes someday to regain enough functioning brain cells to write and publish more broadly and often.

My Pregnant Nose

 Kate Parlin

"Oh my god it smells awful in here! It smells like hair, and dogs, and old feet, and a little like, ew, hummus, maybe? Why does it smell so gross in our bedroom!? Are we gross? Have we always been gross and I just never realized it before? Ugh! I can't take it! I'm getting out of here."

With that, I dragged my ridiculous S-shaped pregnancy pillow down the hall and set up camp in the guest room.

Until that point, I had happily shared a bedroom with my husband and two dogs. It was not especially dirty or gross. I had just finished up my first trimester of pregnancy with twins, and my nose had jumped on the bandwagon of betrayal with so many other parts of my body, making me suffer in weird and unexpected ways.

Thanks, pregnancy hormones. Thanks a lot.

This new, super-sensitive nose of mine also gave me grief at work. I was teaching high school English, stuck in close quarters every day with teenagers whose own powerful hormones combined in a bewildering brew of candy-scented hand cream and neglected hygiene.

Everyone knows about the nausea and vomiting that often accompany pregnancy. But I was not at all prepared for the fresh hell of an over-achieving sense of smell. I was like a dog, distracted by every stinky thing wafting about in the air. Why did dogs seem to think this was so awesome?

My own dogs love nothing more than to get their noses all up inside a pile of trash. They drink it in. They roll in it to get the stench of old Parmesan cheese and bacon grease all over themselves. Every now and then, they manage to get into a trash bag and gleefully strew nastiness all over the kitchen floor. Cleaning it up is one of the most disgusting aspects of dog ownership.

Well, it was. Until I got pregnant. And my dog almost killed both of us.

At the end of a long day, weary from grading essays and ready to put my feet up, I headed home. Oh, how I looked forward to sinking onto the sofa. I pulled into the garage, ready for comfy sweats and possibly a nap. It's remarkably easy to nap when you're pregnant. Once the baby arrives, napping is pretty much all over for the mom, but pregnant naps were the best.

I unlocked the door and pushed it open. The air punched me in the face. Holy. Shit.

The dogs didn't greet me, cheerful tails wagging, like they usually did. They must have sensed my horror. They shrank back and skulked around. It didn't matter that only one dog was actually guilty here; all dogs feel guilty when the owner is mad.

It was everywhere: at least a dozen disgusting piles of poop. I didn't want it to be real. I couldn't breathe, or think, or move.

Was it possible that I could just go right back out the door and run away forever? That actually seemed like a decent solution. I would just get the heck out of there and my husband (possibly with the help of FEMA, or at least a hazmat suit) could deal with this when he got home. Yes! That was a good plan! A great plan!

But he wouldn't be home for another couple of hours. And I really wanted that nap.

Dammit, dogs!

Apparently, while I had been at work shaping young minds and trying not to dry-heave, one of my dogs was up to some horrible, awful, bowel-evacuating mischief. I bet it started with some gurgling in her tummy. I'm sure she started pacing. I imagine that her thoughts went something like this:

Shit. I probably shouldn't have eaten that glob I found in the woods last night. I didn't really know what it was, but it smelled freaking awesome. This is not good. Something very, very bad is going to happen. And here it comes … oh no oh no oh no oh no … and now I'm pooping all over the floor! And again! I can't stop! Oh, they're going to be so mad. They're going to do the thing with the pointy finger and they're going to say "bad dog" and I hate it when they do that, but oh no, oh no, oh no, it's happening and I can't make it stop!! I can't stop pooping! So. Much. Pooping!!!

Can you even imagine what the poor other dog was thinking while all of this was going on? There he was, stuck in the dining room, helplessly watching the Feces Freak poop in circles like a maniac with a broken butt. How he must have hated his life.

Not nearly as much as I hated mine, though, when I finally accepted that there was no way around it. I was in the house. The poop was in the house. We could not co-exist. Time to do this.

I armed myself with rubber gloves and every cleaning product we owned. The stench burrowed into my brain and I was gagging before I even began. I threw the dogs outside and started cleaning. Some of the piles required intense scrubbing and I considered sacrificing a spatula to the cause, but that made me think of poop-pancakes and I had to run to the bathroom to vomit.

I heaved. I cried. I cursed the dogs for being so gross and my husband for not having to deal with this. I considered never letting the dogs back inside. It was a dark, dark time.

When it was all over, when I had lit candles, and sprayed Febreze, and waved burning sage around to chase the poop devils out of every corner, I let the dogs back in. I knew which dog was the culprit, because she was the only one who didn't know better than to gobble down disgusting discoveries in the woods. She stuck to the edges of the room as she walked past me, tail between her legs, with her sorrowful eyebrows up and woeful ears down.

I sighed. I couldn't stay mad at her forever. She didn't mean to poop with a force that threatened to destroy the universe. I called her over, rubbed her ears, and told her I loved her.

I didn't know it then, but that day, the day of the Horrible, Awful Poopcident, marked the beginning of the end of my dog's life as she knew it. My pregnancy was changing my relationship with her, and it would only get worse when not one but two babies arrived to take up all of my attention. Her status in the family would soon be dramatically lowered, and her stinkiness would become the least of my concerns.

But that evening, as I settled onto the sofa for my much-anticipated nap, my little dog snuggled up beside me, happy to be back in my good graces. Exhausted from our traumatic experience, we both slept the deep, peaceful sleep of napping dogs and pregnant women.

Well, at least until my husband came home and started cooking.

"Oh my god, are you making chicken? It smells so gross in this house! Who even eats chicken, anyway? Gah! I can't take it! I'm getting out of here."

Kate Parlin

Kate Parlin is a writer and mother of three girls, two of whom are twins. She is a former high school English teacher who now uses her love of words to chronicle her parenting adventures—the funny, the frustrating, and the infuriating—at her blog, ShakespearesMom.com. Her writing has been featured online at *The Huffington Post*, *The Mid*, *Scary Mommy*, *Mom Babble*, and *Redbook*, and in print in *Pregnancy and Newborn Magazine*, and the Australian publication, *Peninsula Kids*. She is also a contributing author in the book *Martinis & Motherhood: Tales of Wonder, Woe & WTF?!?* She lives in Maine with her husband, their gaggle of girls, and two ridiculous dogs.

The Eviction Notice, Back Labor, and Retribution

 Chris Dean

9:30 am: "I lied!" I cried. Then, the gates of hell opened and the voice of Satan himself emerged from my mouth, "I want an epidural and I want it now!"

The nurse smiled sweetly as she informed me, "Oh honey, it's too late. The baby's crowning!"

"Then take your fucking thumb and push him back in until I get my drugs!"

The nurse actually chuckled when she said, "I'll tell the doctor we're about to have a baby."

She will never know how lucky she was I couldn't roll off the bed and chase her down. Partially because I was hooked up to the human equivalent of a seismograph, but mainly because the next wave of contractions chose that moment to thwart my plans for retribution.

Fifteen hours earlier: It was Halloween and I took my eighteen month old trick-or-treating at the mall. He ran, he wanted to be carried, my back cramped. For almost two hours we replayed this pattern to the point that three different Good Samaritans offered to call an ambulance, since I'm obviously in labor. *I wish!*

Actually, by my records, baby number two was three weeks past the end of his lease on my Mommy Cave. I had used that extra time wisely by trying everything any Old Wife has told me worked for her, her sister, or the friend of a friend of her Great Aunt Gladys, to officially serve the eviction notice.

My best friend took me off-roading in a Jeep with less than zero suspension. We caught some sweet air, but the only thing it brought on was the need to change my underwear. (Because pregnancy bladder doesn't know what fun is.)

We even went on a two-hour hike that involved climbing over fallen trees and boulders, most of it with an eighteen month old alternating between hanging on my back like a possum and sitting on the baby bump like a boss. I came away exhausted and with a mild case of poison ivy, but no friggin' baby!

By then I'd made peace with the fact that the kid wasn't coming out until he was old enough to walk out of the hospital holding my hand. So of course, back spasms weren't any big deal.

We ran (and waddled) the candy gauntlet, then decided to take our tired selves home for a bath and a bedtime story for the munchkin and a long rock in a relaxing chair for my back.

4:00 am: I woke up with an uncharacteristic clarity of mind that told me the back spasms hadn't really been spasms at all, but the harbingers of a much bigger bodily storm—that which is known as Son-of-a-bitch-I'm-in-labor!

As gently as was possible, I shook Hubby awake and lovingly whispered, "Wake up you bastard, I'm having your baby!"

To which he sweetly replied, "One more hour," and resumed his snoring.

Okay, fine. I got this. I mean, it wasn't like it was my first rodeo and baby number one had taken almost twenty hours to finally make his appearance. So, I used my hour to fold some laundry, double check my bag for the hospital, and wake my mom to tell her I was in labor. "Bring me home a beautiful baby girl," was her send-off.

Dead on the sixty-minute mark, I climbed onto the bed, one thunderous tree-trunk leg on either side of Hubby's torso, and I jumped like our eighteen month old while screaming, "Can we go to the hospital now!?"

He opened one eye, looked up nervously and replied, "You were serious? Why didn't you wake me up!?"

Okay, just kiddin'. It wasn't said gently, it was panic-screamed.

Anyway, we would have made it to the hospital in record time if it wasn't for the fact that Mr. Genius had to stop for a soda. But he wasn't being totally selfish, which he proved by handing me a can of cream soda and a candy bar as he climbed back in the car. Because what woman in hard labor doesn't need a sugar rush to fuel her contractions?

We made it through check-in without me so much as yelling at him, let alone threatening to rip anything off. So I was doing great! I was escorted to my labor room, hooked up to the fancy machinery, and given the first of somewhere around fifty pelvic exams. Yep, everything was going according to plan and I was hanging in there like a pro.

Okay, I was a sweaty mess with a very thin perma-smile slapped on, but I was uncharacteristically non-violent. Right up until Dr. Brilliant casually mentioned, "Well, you're dilating beautifully, but your water hasn't broken. Why don't we help things along and take care of that for you?" The last part must have been a rhetorical question, since I didn't have time to share my thoughts on water breakage before I felt a tiny pinch followed by me wetting the bed. Then all hell broke loose in my uterus.

The machinery that, up to this point had spit out graphs consisting of smooth ups-and-downs, now began to jump around like a lie detector hooked up to a politician.

"Wow!" I turned my head enough to see who the hell was stupid enough to sound that damn perky in my presence, only to see Hubby staring at the monitor. "That was a big one!"

There may or may not have been a mad grab at his manhood while the voice of Satan returned, uttering all manner of graphic threats. Hubby dodged left and was smart enough to remain out of my reach the rest of the morning. And by out of my reach, I mean he turned the TV on and busied himself with watching Star Trek reruns. (Note to self: Spend the next ten years never letting him forget this error in judgement.)

9:30 am, revisited: Dr. Brilliant walked in, donned her miner's hat with the adorable little light, and began surveying my cervix.

"It appears he's crowned!"

"So I've heard. Now, push him back in and Give. Me. My. Drugs!"

"Ha, ha, ha. We're a little past that now. You're about to be a mommy!"

"I'm already a mommy. What I want to be is drugged!"

As you can probably guess, my demands for an epidural were ignored, including the part of the day when the baby decided to finally make his dramatic entrance.

But all the Old Wives were right about one thing—it really is the most forgettable pain. When I was shown the tiny, messy face of the beautiful baby boy that had been giving his all to come out after three weeks of giving his all to stay in, the previous sixteen hours were completely forgotten.

And that cream soda and candy bar I'd had on the drive in? Well, let's just say that the nurse who'd not only refused to push the kid back in, but had then added insult to injury by laughing at me? By chance alone she ended up on the receiving end of its glorious return the moment I started to push.

Looks like I had my retribution after all!

Chris Dean

Chris Dean writes at www.PixieCD.com, where she shares acts of stupidity, life with adult offspring, and the occasional useful bit of info on life with chronic illness. Her work has appeared on *The Huffington Post, Scary Mommy, In The Powder Room, Bonbon Break,* and *Midlife Boulevard*, as well as in print in *Clash of the Couples*. Chris lives in Indiana with her amazingly tolerant Hubby, their four adult kids, and the petting zoo full of cats, dogs, chickens, Muscovy ducks, and geese she's systematically managed to turn their home and yard into. When not writing, you can find her avoiding laundry on social media.

Pregnantpause

 Lucia Paul

While I was pregnant with my son, I was thirty-five-years old. Today, of course, that seems like the fresh blush of youth. But sixteen years ago, it was akin to having been a worker in the original Ford Automotive Plant. I was a curiosity. An old timer. At least at the obstetrician's office. My first lengthy discussion of menopause actually took place somewhere in my final trimester of pregnancy.

In 1998, at least around here, they stamped my chart with "elderly gravidas," which I took at first to be a huge compliment. "She's got a lot of gravitas. She's very, very intelligent." Well, that's what I imagined they were saying when anyone took a look at my chart. Turns out (and yes, clearly I am not in the medical profession) it means something like "advanced maternal age."

Not very flattering. At least not to me. Today, it's no big deal whatsoever to have baby number one at forty. But back in the day, they acted like Betty White was sporting a maternity jumper whenever I showed up for an appointment.

Perhaps you'll join me in my feeling that while in an advanced pregnant state, focusing on the inevitability of menopause and perimenopause for that matter, was a bit strange.

At that appointment in 1998, I was full of wacky questions like, "Why are my ankles filled with what appear to be water wings?" And, "Should I be having shooting pains from my shoulders to my toes day and night?" But the doctor I saw that day was intent on getting me up to speed on menopause.

"Well, I see here that you are thirty five years old, hm." She looked at her clipboard. No modern, hand-held, nifty computer. This was still "pens on paper" in the doctor's office.

"We really need to discuss menopause, and what we like to call, perimenopause."

I shifted a bit on the examining table so she could see the large lump I was currently sporting under my actual epidermis. But ever a pleaser, I tried to be upbeat.

"Well, ha, ha, you see I'm actually pregnant right now. So it seems we might be putting the cart before the horse. You could actually put me before the horse and I could probably pull a fairly large wagon." I felt I was quite jolly.

She gave me the "I'm a science person, not a people person," look that I have come to know so well in doctor's offices. But that's never stopped me. I continued.

"Call me crazy, but while actually 'with child' I feel kind of fertile. Sort of as if, well, I'm a ways off from menopause." I chuckled warmly in an attempt to get her to join me. No such luck.

She turned and grabbed a pamphlet from the neat arrangement on the wall. The wooden rack held many pamphlets with comforting titles like, "Uterine Prolapse: Friend or Foe?" "The Wonderful Mystery of Bladder Leakage" and "Your Journey with Warts." She handed me "Perimenopause: Precursor to the Change."

As I struggled to a sitting position (pregnant!) and adjusted my Old Navy (maternity!) top, she remained cool. Not to mention fairly uninterested in my maternal state. I was now feeling irked. Pissed is synonymous with irked, right?

I took the pamphlet, glanced quickly at it, and cavalierly put it face down on the tiny bit of my lap that was left.

"Well, I have never heard of perimenopause," I said, because I actually hadn't. Remember, this was the late nineties. We still had CD players and a large collection of VHS tapes. Plus I was in my fertile years. I was pregnant for the love of Pete. Why not start talking about my funeral arrangements or reverse mortgage?

She was used to non-sciencey people such as myself.

"We have identified that the ten to fifteen years that precede menopause have their own set of physical changes," she told me calmly.

"Well, let's get a group of nineteen year olds in here and start jawing about it! Ten to fifteen years? I say let's bundle the two to three decades before menopause all together! We'll call it 'Your-Entire-Adult-Life-As-a-Woman-is-the-Time-Before-Menopause' Pause." Man, I'm good.

"Now you're just being silly," she said. The only thing that got her to take my actual pregnancy seriously was when I switched the topic to the Braxton Hicks contractions I had been having for weeks. That means I personally had to scare her off the topic of menopause. You've got to fight fire with fire, I say.

Happily, I only had another month of pregnancy to ponder my impending crone status, because I gave birth to my darling boy a few weeks before his due date. I now think of that as "Two extra weeks of perimenopause."

Why wouldn't I?

Lucia Paul

Lucia Paul's humor writing includes an award-winning sitcom script and essays that have appeared in numerous publications. She is a regular humor contributor to online sites including *The Erma Bombeck Writer's Workshop* and *Midlife Boulevard*, on topics ranging from the financial crisis to parenting teens. She has stories and essays in multiple anthologies including, *Motherhood May Cause Drowsiness: Funny Stories by Sleepy Moms*. Find her at DysfunctionalScrapbooking.blogspot.com.

The Queen of Thrones

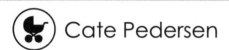 Cate Pedersen

It wasn't so much the hemorrhoids or the burning when I urinated; it wasn't really the fact that I was awoken from a borderline comatose slumber several times a night; and it certainly wasn't the feeling that my body no longer belonged to me. It was all of it combined. The humiliating, soul-sucking days right after giving birth that had me saying, "Maybe one is enough. Yeah, definitely. I know I was insistent I wanted four children, but really, look at this place. There's no room for more than one child."

I was exhausted during those first days at home after being shoved out into the cold night after less than twenty-four hours in the hospital. Okay, I had insisted on going home. I couldn't stand one more minute of mewling babes that weren't my own, and nurses that kept sneaking off with my baby as soon as I nodded off. I woke to find the bassinet gone from my room, and stumbled down the hall to catch a guilty looking nurse forcing a soother into my baby's mouth—after I specifically said no to bottles and soothers. And so as soon as I could be released, my husband helped me pack up and get our family back home.

But home was not the haven I'd hoped for. I felt like a stranger in a strange land. I felt rather let down by this whole motherhood hype, actually. I had planned my daughter's birth almost down to the day, and counted back carefully to make sure I conceived at the perfect time. I had been the sustainable momma (okay, I was cheap) and bought all second-hand furniture, and graciously accepted hand-me-down clothes. I even took up crocheting to make my first thing ever—a baby blanket for my sweet angel. I organized the nursery and scrubbed and cleaned everything so that all would be ready when I came home from the hospital with my bundle of joy.

I imagined that I would be kick ass at this mothering thing because of my years babysitting and going soft every time I saw a dimpled cheek. I always envied the women with strollers jammed with toddlers, and had a hard time passing the baby back to its mother at baby showers. I was meant to be a mom and couldn't wait for my turn. Had I been able to preview the first week at home after having a human being wrenched from my innards, I think I might have opted to adopt a puppy instead.

There is nothing warm and fuzzy about dozing off with an infant attached to your breast who is covered in peas and rice from the take-out Chinese food your supportive husband ordered in lieu of the promised home-cooked meal. And the stench of a full diaper genie mixed with the aroma of a moist pile of laundry is not the powder-scented heaven I had imagined life with baby would be.

My saving grace was my parents who showed up mid-week to help with the housework and cuddle the baby while I tried to sleep. But no one told me about the manic wakefulness you can experience after having a baby. I could not sleep unless she was right next to me, so the beautiful nursery went unused and the help from the grandparents was unappreciated. I could only sleep when she slept. My brain was on overdrive and every sound was like cannon shot. When I did sleep, I jolted awake and lay there, staring at a shadowy figure in the doorway holding my baby upside-down in the air. My worn out brain was hallucinating, and the instinctive mother lion that had lain dormant was pacing around inside me.

I thought I was going mad. It was a good week before I was able to sleep soundly and my emotions settled.

For instance, I mourned my body as if I had lost a loved one. I wanted to curl up in a corner, and lick my wounds, and growl at anyone who came close. In fact, I think I may have done that once or twice—my memory is a bit foggy. In retrospect, I should have had a funeral for my pre-baby body. "Here lies the mutilated corpse that was once a firm and shapely form. Oh, we shall remember the breasts that sat so high and perky, now swollen from milk and misshapen. We shall rejoice in the memory of smooth skin, now crisscrossed with scar tissue and stretch marks. We shall recall a time without anal fissures and pain that cuts like a knife when pooping." My poor body. I don't think anyone who hasn't experienced childbirth can understand the discomfort women suffer to the delicate parts of their bodies. I could only urinate in the shower as I was terrified of the searing pain. And I don't even want to think about the drama around going number two!

But I will think about it. Going to the bathroom was a major event. It took scheduling, moral support, research, and equipment. My arsenal was a bowl and Epsom salts for soaking, baby wipes and cool compresses, squeezy bottles for washing, anesthetic sprays and aloe vera gels, a doughnut cushion for sitting on and, oh, the gooey mess that is supposed to shrink the evil devils—the dreaded hemorrhoid creams and suppositories. I had a love–hate relationship with the toilet. We bonded and I poured out my heart and soul to that cold waste receptacle. I spent so much time in the bathroom I began to get territorial. Give me a scepter and a crown and call it a day; I was an unwilling monarch on my porcelain throne.

It took three weeks before I could go to the bathroom without my eyes watering, and did that ever feel like a victory! The toilet bowl and I rejoiced. But it was not a victory without some blows to my honor and self-respect. One specific moment will be emblazoned in memory forever. It had been a particularly restless night, and I had dragged myself into the bathroom and almost dozed off on my friend, the toilet. I thought a nice tooth-brushing and face-washing would liven me up a little, so I squeezed the toothpaste onto my brush and scrubbed at my scum-coated teeth. It took a while before I noticed I was not enjoying the refreshing minty taste I was hoping to experience. I pulled the toothbrush from my mouth and stared at it for a moment before accepting that it did not look like toothpaste on the bristles. My gaze drifted sideways to the tube beside the sink, which was clearly labeled as an ointment for the ass, and not a cleanser for the mouth. I think an incident like this must have sparked the phrase "Mommy Brain." I spent more time scrubbing out my mouth that day than I ever did before or since. Women with pregnancy brain should not operate machinery or tools, including toothbrushes.

I may never have gotten over the teeth-brushing incident, but I got over everything else. We women are strong, fierce creatures who can get through anything. And I would do it all again to have the privilege of being mother to my two (yes, I went through all this a second time), gorgeous children who are the light of my life. And the toilet and I have a healthy relationship once more.

Cate Pedersen

Cate Pedersen is a freelance writer and editor, a fantasy/sci-fi author, and—last but not least—a mother to teenagers. She mentions motherhood last as she sometimes hopes to avoid the hefty weight she feels bearing down as she rushes to finish raising them before they are released into an unprepared world. Cate knows the experience of being a mother cannot be described by one person, and can never be captured in one moment, but all of the "mom"ents together make up the whole messy, painful, wonderful, funny, spiritual adventure that is motherhood. Cate wants to thank her two children who have provided her with a never-ending supply of fodder for embarrassing stories, but she may have to wait until she is living on a different continent before sharing all the stories in print—if she survives the teenage years!

Are You Shitting Me?

The Things They Never Tell You About Childbirth

 Megan Woolsey

During my first pregnancy, the embryo ended up attaching itself to my bladder. It required surgery for removal. I didn't even know such a thing could happen, but since it had taken me a year to get pregnant I was just happy to know that there were viable eggs in my body.

A year and a half later, I got pregnant with a baby that chose to travel where she was supposed to, ending up in my uterus where she grew beyond her acceptable due date.

I went in to the hospital to deliver this child with the help of some drugs to speed the process along, because she had stayed a week past her due date. I sat in my hospital bed at 7 am and watched the Pitocin drip slowly into my arm. The nurse had done a real bang-up job of putting the IV needle in my hand, so it was throbbing.

There are certain things that nobody tells you when you go in to have a baby. The first thing nobody told me is that once they hook you up with all the drugs and start your labor process, you are not allowed to eat. By 8 am I was so hungry I was ready to eat a full spaghetti meal with a side slab of beef. Instead, the nurses offered me ice chips.

My mom showed up to the hospital and parked her Porsche. As the contractions started to grip my abdomen, I watched through the window as my mother painstakingly covered every inch of her pristine Porsche with the custom made vinyl car cover. I was annoyed. I was just starting to feel the effects of labor. My mind started spinning with the reality of what a life-changing day I was about to have and my mom was super worried about tree debris falling on her car in the hospital parking lot.

By lunchtime I was beside myself with hunger. I was ravenous. A hungry pregnant woman in labor is a recipe for disaster. Then my husband and mom began discussing what they were going to eat for lunch. They decided on Mexican food, my personal favorite delicacy. It was intolerable having to listen to these two people who were supposed to love me more than anyone on this earth talk about what they were eating for lunch while I sat there in labor, absolutely starving. It was even worse when they showed up with their plates of nachos oozing with cheesy goodness and refried beans piled high, and proceeded to eat it in front of me. I felt like jumping out of my hospital bed and beating them with the pole my Pitocin drip was hanging from. But I didn't.

The second thing nobody shared with me about the delivery process is that I would need to reach a certain dilation before I got to receive the beloved epidural. I spent most of the day dilated to three, even though I really needed to be closer to ten to be eligible for pain relief. When I finally reached the magic number, a really tall, dark and handsome anesthesiologist came in the room to administer my pain meds. He came equipped with a big ass needle that was slated to go right into my spine. Unfortunately, my anesthesiologists' good looks were his best asset since his job skills were questionable. It turns out he was quite new at this important job of pain management for women in labor. He poked and moved the needle around in my spine. He started to sweat and asked my husband to turn his camera off. I looked at the nurses holding me down by my shoulders and they returned the look with nervousness. A half an hour later he had the epidural in and the relief started to wash over my body.

By 10 pm I was still in labor, I was still starving, and I was still being fed ice chips. I invited both of my parents and husband in the room to experience the magic of childbirth.

I opted to have the big, full-length mirror placed at my feet so I could watch my child emerging from my body. Why that sounded like a good idea, I have no idea. Before labor, it sounded super cool and very forward thinking to put a gigantic full size mirror in front of my va-jay-jay for my own personal peep show. It turns out pushing a baby out of your vagina is a little stressful and there was very little time to gaze at my private area in hopes that one day a baby would emerge. Plus, because of this mirror, I ended up seeing things I never needed to see, which leads me to the third thing nobody told me about.

I was concentrating on pushing so hard because I was completely done with this childbirth shit. That is when I saw it. The third thing nobody told me would happen during childbirth. I had read so many baby books and nowhere did they mention this horrible truth.

I looked closer in the mirror and discovered in horror that I had lost control of my faculties. It was happening right there in the delivery room in front of nurses, doctors, my parents and my husband. I guess if you are pushing that hard from your abdomen, you are bound to lose something. But after twelve hours of labor, my embarrassment over this circumstance was temporary.

After getting over the horror of losing my bowels with my legs splayed open in front of family and strangers, I started really focusing on getting my child out. Things weren't looking good and there was threat of a C-section. I had worked hard all day at giving birth the vaginal way and the last thing I wanted was to be sliced open and have my organs moved out in order to have this baby.

My baby, Ava, was finally born and she was pissed. Once they poked and prodded her to the point where she actually bled, they bathed her. She was so cold that she shivered and cried. I already felt mom guilt that my baby was thrust into this world and already facing challenges. It was just the beginning.

I was one of those moms who had a five-page manual with very strict birthing instructions. A pointless waste of trees that was. I don't think my husband and I followed a single one of my perfect rules I had laid out for this birthing process, except maybe the one where we play our favorite music from a playlist I made. I was only a mom for a few hours and already I was breaking my own rules. I saw right away how this mom thing was going to be.

One of my most important requirements was that my baby never leave my side. She would stay in my room with me the entire time we were in the hospital and I would nurse her and we would be peaceful and happy.

The first opportunity I got, I kicked my baby right out of the room. I rang the nurse to take my screaming child and keep her busy in the nursery so I could sleep. Oh, and if at all possible, please don't give her a binky, I said half-heartedly. I really didn't give two shits about binkies at that point. I did care about eating some greasy Mexican food and sleeping though the night.

I can't say that childrearing has been much easier than the birthing process, but I will say it really can't be that bad since we all keep doing it. Three years later I had triplets. That time I went straight to the C-section, but I ate some nachos first.

Megan Woolsey

Megan Woolsey lives in beautiful Northern California with her family of six, including triplets and a vivacious big sister. With three redheads in the family, life around her home is never dull. Megan is passionate about travel, finds peace in yoga, and is always on the lookout for a nice bottle of Zin that doesn't render a hangover. Her goal in life is to be a travel writer. Megan Woolsey authors the blog, TheHipMothership.com, and has been published on *The Huffington Post, Scary Mommy, Mamalode, BLUNTmoms, Bonbon Break, Role Reboot,* and *Erma Bombeck's Writer's Workshop.* When Megan needs a break from the kids, you can find her perusing her social media pages.

Humpty Dumpty, Dissolvable Stitches, and 'No Chance Underpants'

 Alice Gomstyn

"The baby did a number on your wife's vagina," is a sentence that could be, if one were inclined to be optimistic (and fairly delusional), interpreted in a pretty festive way. By "did a number," perhaps my obstetrician, who said this rather casually to my bewildered husband, meant that the 7 pound, 9 ounce critter that wriggled out of me happened to perform a quick tap dance routine along the way—a showy little shuffle-hop-step somewhere in between my uterus and the doctor's waiting hands, his tiny feet endowed with tap shoes that I must have accidentally and unknowingly sat on sometime during my pregnancy. A lot can happen on a crowded subway car.

In reality, the obstetrician was referring to the fact that my future Fred Astaire, while making his grand debut, managed to cause a tear through the muscles just behind my vagina. It was why, after he came out at the end of an exhausting, day-long labor, I was forced to lie with my knees spread painfully far apart for what felt like an eternity. All I wanted to do was close my legs, goddamn it, but no! The doctor stubbornly insisted on stitching me back into shape.

At the time, I found this highly annoying, but in hindsight, I give her oodles of credit since the aforementioned stitching took place in such a complicated area. After all, each woman's vagina is its own unique, special snowflake, is it not? I think OB/GYNs are already widely respected, but however much appreciation they get, it's still not enough. If Humpty Dumpty were a she, I'm quite certain any competent OB/GYN could have deftly put her weirdo eggy body back together again, and then nonchalantly mention to all the king's horses and all the king's men, "Boy, that great fall did a number on your egg's vagina."

I'll admit I wasn't prepared for the physical aftermath of childbirth. Sure, thanks to educational films such as *Look Who's Talking* and *Nine Months*, I knew that labor itself would be excruciatingly painful (and, potentially, full of hilarious sight gags). But the recovery afterward? The prolific bleeding? The dissolvable sutures? The analgesic creams and numbing sprays? The terror of that first, postpartum, "please don't let me poop off my stitches" bowel movement? Why hasn't anyone made a movie about that? Or, if not a movie, how about a song? Something modeled on "You Are My Sunshine" could work. My suggested lyrics: "You are my vagina, my torn vagina. You birthed a baby, now you are frayed."

I came to learn that my tearing was considered a second degree laceration, meaning that it was more painful than the first degree type (which I inexpertly imagine to be something akin to a paper cut) but better than the third- and fourth-degree kind, which to my understanding amounts to the outgoing baby playing *Wreck-It Ralph* on your sphincter.

Though my injury was on the more benign side of the spectrum, it didn't save me from some three weeks of sizeable discomfort. Standing for long periods of time was out, as was sitting on anything harder than a marshmallow. Fortunately, the hospital provided me with a two-foot-by-two-foot foam eggshell cushion in my post-delivery goody bag.

Also included in the bag was the least sexy mesh underwear you could ever imagine and, curiously, a pair of ear plugs. It's as if the wise and sympathetic folks at the hospital gift department were none-too-subtly telegraphing to me that I should go ahead and start ignoring my baby's cries early—waiting for the three-month mark to do sleep training is for sissies!—and, while I'm at it, ensure even more sleep by eliminating any possibility of my husband craving coitus from yours truly, thanks, of course, to the hospital-grade granny panties.

If I were a hospital administrator and the budget was tight, I might consider rationing the mood-killing underpants and providing them only to the most annoying or unpleasant patients, making their return to the delivery ward far less likely, for example, "We thought we'd have another child, but at the sight of my underwear, my husband retreated to the edge of the bed and didn't roll back over until well after I hit menopause." Perhaps a savvy marketer could turn a real profit off the product, selling it to the masses so that women could have a sex discouragement strategy less clichéd than just whipping out the ol' "I have a headache" excuse. All a company would need is a catchy name for the underwear, like "No Chance Underpants" or "Whore No More Lady Shorts." Your move, Hanes.

But the hospital eggshell cushion was far and away the most crucial parting gift. It quickly found itself a home on one of our dining room chairs and when friends came over for dinner, they soon discovered which chair was indisputably mine for the sitting. You might think I would have been embarrassed by my bright blue foam friend, but it was very much the opposite—I was exceedingly proud of it. It helped me announce to the world, "I valiantly withstood twenty-one hours of childbirth and have the sore genitals to prove it!" Try fitting that on a T-shirt. (No, seriously, try it. Then send it to me. Ladies' size medium. Cotton-lycra blend, if possible. Thanks.)

Apparently, for all my pain, I didn't do nearly enough complaining to adequately convey my bodily misery. I say this because at one point, about a week after the delivery, my husband didn't think twice of griping to me how much he dreaded peeling off of his arm a small bandage covering a cut he got while gardening.

"It's going to hurt so much because it's sticking to the hairs on my arm," he said, his widened eyes begging for sympathy.

I stared at him blankly for a minute and then replied, "I have stitches in my vagina."

He quickly dropped the subject.

Alice Gomstyn

Alice Gomstyn is a freelance journalist, blogger, humorist, and mildly inappropriate mommy to two spirited little boys. A former digital reporter for ABC News and current contributor to Babble.com, she's covered business, health, education, and parenting. Check out her personal parenting observations, usually in the form of absurd wisecracks, at MildlyInappropriateMommy.com.

10 Ways to Know You Aren't Done Having Kids

 Amanda Mushro

When I'm out at Target for the 347th time in one month, I can always count on a few things happening:

I will not make it out of the store spending less than $100. I have heard this is possible, but I believe this to be an urban legend much like Big Foot or the newborn that sleeps through the night.

Even though I swore, pre-children, I would never be one of "those" mothers that feed their children with the unpaid snacks that fill their cart, I'm usually ripping open the crackers and chips with my teeth if it means five more minutes of $1 bin shopping. "The audacity of those women," I would scoff. "Feed your kid before you get into the store." Poor, naïve, childless me, how could I have known that those unpaid Goldfish served as bribery and sources of entertainment and not nutrition?

Someone will say to me, "Oh you have a boy and a girl! How lucky for you! You can be done having kids now."

Excuse me, random stranger? Are you part of the fertility police? Apparently I've won uterus roulette, and after birthing a male and a female, my lady parts become non-functional and while the playground is open, the merry-go-round is closed.

But that's the thing, I don't know if we are meant to be a party of four or a party of five. These days I feel like everyone around me is pregnant and seeing so many pregnant women can be dangerous for a girl like me. Right now I have a biological clock that is shouting "tick, tick, tick, boom—dynamite." Part of me can't help but look at our dinner table and wonder if someone is missing.

To be honest, I change my mind based on the day. If the kids are being good and one of them does something particularly sweet or adorable—it's a three-kid kind of day. If someone throws a tantrum, I can't remember the last time I showered uninterrupted, or my husband works late—two-kid day.

Deciding to add to your brood can be a difficult decision, but luckily for you, I have devised a simple quiz to help you determine if you can expect a bun in your oven in the near future. So if you are teetering between going from one to two, or you're doing it hoping for bambino number 20, all you need is a simple answer of "yes" or "no" for each statement. For every yes, give yourself a point.

1. While sitting among the ladies waiting for a pap smear at your yearly exam, you longingly look across the waiting room at the pregnant women and wish you were "playing for the other team."

2. When you hold someone else's baby, your ovaries make an actual sound, and it sounds a lot like a sad trombone.

3. And when it is time for you to hand that baby back to her mama, you held on just a little too long, took too many sniffs of that babe's head, and got dubbed that "crazy baby sniffer."

4. The movie *Frozen* has totally traumatized you, and not because your kid has sung "Let It Go" approximately three million times in your car, but because every time

that boat goes down with the parents aboard, you panic thinking your kid will want to build a snowman and have no one to ride bikes with around the halls.

5. You have baby names already picked out and if someone on Facebook uses that name for their kid, you refer to them as "name-stealer" or "worst-friend-ever." You also make outlandish claims that their baby looks a lot like Sonny Bono.

6. You have a secret board on Pinterest where you pin ways to announce a new pregnancy and when the sweet bundle of joy arrives. Plus you really want to have a gender reveal party because they're just cool and they didn't have those cool things the last time you were pregnant. All you had was a blurry sonogram, and if there wasn't an arrow pointing to your kids junk, you'd have no idea if it was a boy or girl. Dammit, you want to cut into a cake or release a few balloons too.

7. Sorting through your kids' piles of outgrown clothes is enough to send you over the edge or face first into a huge glass of wine. You cannot bear to part with any of their tiny shoes or soft blankets. Currently your two-car garage is feeling the squeeze and you might not get your swagger wagon inside if you don't make some decisions.

8. You just got a "save the date" for your cousin's wedding that is happening on a beautiful tropical island next year, and you're just not sure you can commit...yet.

9. You spent last weekend "cleaning up" the guest room. Possibly measuring to see if a crib would fit against that wall and maybe a rocking chair over in that corner.

10. You've started to kid yourself that the awful side effects of pregnancy really aren't so wretched. "Morning sickness? Oh it wasn't that bad!" "I really can function on a lot less sleep than the average person." "Labor and delivery? 'Tis but a scratch!"

Results:

0 points. We get it, you're done. Done. You've sent your husband off to the guillotine for his little snip-snip and you tossed out the baby bibs as soon as your last kid could wipe their own face.

1–3 points. You may have thought about having another kid, but then your current children performed their magic (tantrum, multiple trips to time out, unexplained substance on the bathroom celling), and they cured your baby fever ASAP. Just find a baby of a family member or neighbor to hold or sniff their head a bit.

4–7 points. You put up a good front, but you could be convinced either way. You've got a mild case of baby fever, but it wouldn't take much for you to "pull the goalie." If you have a vacation, a blizzard, or a few too many drinks one night, you should fully expect to be knocked up. Be prepared.

8–10 points. Come on, who are you kidding? You already have one leg up in the stirrups.

Amanda Mushro

Amanda Mushro is the writer behind the blog QuestionableChoicesInParenting.com. Sometimes she thinks she is doing a great job as a mom, but then she does something that makes her question her own parenting abilities. She lives in Maryland with her husband and kids and tries every day to laugh at life as a parent so they don't commit her. She has been featured on *The TODAY Show*, Today.com, *Scary Mommy*, and *The Huffington Post*. She is the director of *Listen to Your Mother: Pittsburgh* and has essays featured in the seven anthologies.

Good Advice

 Megan Steusloff

When I was pregnant with my first child, I had my friends and family compile a small book of advice. In addition to reading every published book on pregnancy and child rearing so that I'd have a healthy, happy, well-adjusted, confident, and polite child, I decided to get more information (and more confusion, for that matter) by requiring this book of advice from my closest allies.

The book of advice made for interesting reading: Every child needs a dog, never put stuffed animals in a crib, when a baby cries sprinkle them with water, never babble or talk "baby talk," paint the nursery green because it is the most soothing of colors, never forget your stroller, bury pennies in the garden and have your child dig for pirate gold, always wear helmets when riding your bike, it is impossible to choke on Cheerios so feed your child Cheerios as often as possible, and never use a nightlight because it encourages fear of the dark, to share a few.

Let's just say that I entered into this pregnancy and parenting adventure with way too much information and such mixed signals and suggestions that I had no idea where to start. Then I read what my parents wrote on the very last page of the little book. It simply stated, "Enjoy this book. Read the advice once, and then forget it. All a parent has to do is follow their own heart, do what feels right for you and your child, and the world will be as it should."

My son and daughter have grown up with two beautiful dogs, but the dogs were my first babies. Neither of my children has ever even slept in a crib. The only time I have sprayed my children with water is in the bathtub or on a hot summer's day, and it has been while they are giggling, definitely not while crying. The nurseries are red and blue; peach and pink, respectively. There was no reason to bury pirate gold because my kids are captivated by seeds and flowers and worms. We are hikers, not bikers. My children do not like Cheerios, or riding in a stroller. They do, however, love their bright blue shimmering star nightlights. We talk and sing and laugh and make all kinds of funny noises together, does that qualify as babbling?

The ironic lesson to be learned is that the best advice I ever received on parenting was to trust my own instincts way more than trusting any advice, no matter who the expert happened to be. Yet, being a parent does make you feel like a connoisseur of sorts, and inspires you to want to pass on your lessons learned to both your own children and to new mothers everywhere.

And so, if some naïve and terrified pregnant woman asks me for advice, this is what I would tell her: love every moment. There will be big, life changing moments like first steps and splashing in the ocean. There will be small, everyday events like spilling peas all over the kitchen floor or reading the same book for the thousandth time before bed. But every moment is building a foundation for this little person who is counting on you. It will be messy and scary and fun. You will cry tears of frustration and exhaustion. You will laugh until you can no longer breathe. You will suddenly begin buckling your seat belt even when you are in the back seat. You'll start picking up litter and donating to charities, because not only do you want the world to be a better place, but you want to hold onto this world that is now home to the most wonderful person in existence, for as long as you can be witness. Enjoy the ride, smile often, notice the details, and remember that this all will pass way too fast. And finally, forget all that I said. You are a mom; all moms know exactly what to do, and somehow even when they don't, they have a way of rising to the occasion.

When it comes to my own little ones, I do like to give advice; I have slightly more to pass on. As a parent you should keep your own counsel most dear, but children sometimes need guidance. This is the advice that I whisper in my children's ears whenever needed:

Be curious! Always wonder and ask lots of questions. Stop to watch and observe the world. I want you to watch ants carry crumbs back to their anthills, and turtles sunning themselves on logs. Imagine yourself as an eagle soaring through the clouds or a dolphin frolicking in the waves. Play hard and pretend and imagine and dream huge dreams. Be an astronaut, chef, farmer, teacher, zoologist, truck driver, construction worker, doctor, rock star, and artist all in the same day. Enjoy nature, and do not miss the opportunity to experience a sunset or a meteorite or a thunderstorm. Read and write to discover yourself and the past, present, and future. Imagination and enthusiasm will bring such happiness to your life. Trust and follow your inner child no matter how old you become.

Be open-minded! Be accepting and tolerant of others, and recognize the strength in diversity. Remember that friendship and love transcend race, age, culture, and gender. Be willing to try new experiences and appreciate the strengths and talents of others. Enjoy a variety of music, read a variety of books, look at art as any form of creative energy that leaves an influence and mark on the world. Listen and look more than judge. Recognize that uniqueness and individuality is invaluable, but so is the ability to be part of a team, learning from and teaching each other. Be positive, and try to see the best in any given situation. Never join the crowd or follow the rules that you know to be wrong, but instead relish and celebrate the goodness of change. You will come across people living in cardboard boxes and others that live in houses that we could not afford if we lived and worked through ten lifetimes. Give them all your eye contact, respect, and a smile. Everyone has a story to tell and something to teach us. Be a beautiful spirit, a revolutionist, and a warrior of hope. Make the world a brighter place by letting your divine spark shine and allowing the inner light of others to shine alongside you.

Be brave! I want you to be courageous! Most of what you worry about never happens, so why waste precious time? I want you to ride roller coasters, swim in oceans, swing for the fence, dance whenever you feel the desire, climb mountains, love wildly, and try everything that you dream of. Be careful and not reckless with your safety (check your seatbelt, watch for sharks, wear a helmet, carry a granola bar in your pocket, etc.), but live freely and with pizzazz! Never be afraid to be different—stand out and be proud—you are the one and only you! It is not about never feeling afraid, and all about facing those fears with faith and vitality and integrity. Mistakes will happen. Failure will haunt you. But try again and again and one more time. Do not let anything stand in your way of doing what you were put here to do. Life is a gift, live it and enjoy it. Take a deep breath and go for it. Let, "I can do this" be your mantra for everything!

Be caring! Think with and listen to your heart at all times. Leave wherever you go a better place than the way you found it. Leave whomever you meet happier than they were before they came in contact with you. Have reverence for life and joy and hope. Be picky when choosing whom to give your love to, but with those you love give it all. Hold doors open for strangers, bake cookies for neighbors, say thank you to everyone that helps you through your day. Remember that everyone has feelings and a heart, so tread gently. Be tender with animals and people and yourself. Be kind to books and ideas and belongings. You never know what may be a treasure in disguise. Love is meaning and purpose and all that will remain at the end.

As time goes by on this journey of parenthood, I sometimes look at that book of advice collecting dust on my bookshelf and smile. I am such a work in progress. I have made whopping mistakes and I have made miracles happen. I have enjoyed perfect calm next to sun kissed kids on sandy beaches, and I have anxiously prayed all night in hospital emergency rooms. I have walls filled with finger-painted masterpieces and scrapbooks stuffed with memories. I am proud, tired, happy, grateful, and thrilled by the thought that the best is yet to come.

Megan Steusloff

Megan Steusloff is happily married and has two beautiful little ones that keep her very busy. Megan is an elementary school reading specialist and freelance writer from Sterling Heights, Michigan. She is a proud graduate of Oakland University, and a self-declared lifelong learner. She loves going on adventures of all sizes with her family, reading, writing, gardening, taking long walks, and traveling. She strives to play, listen, explore, imagine, dream, create, and laugh every day with her wonderful students and her own amazing kids.

Author Social Media Appendix

Lynn Adams

Twitter.com/AdamsLynnphd

Christina Antus

Facebook.com/ChristinaAntusWriter

Jessica Azar

Facebook.com/HerdManagement

Twitter.com/jazar31583

Pinterest.com/JessicaAzar

Emily Ballard

Facebook.com/EmilyRVBallard

Pinterest.com/EmilyBallard

Instagram.com/EmilyRVBallard

Teri Biebel

Facebook.com/SnarkfestBlog

Twitter.com/SnarkfestBlog

Pinterest.com/Snarkfest

Richard Black

Facebook.com/Unfit.Father

Twitter.com/TheUnfitFather

Sarah Bregel

Facebook.com/TheMediocreMama

Twitter.com/SarahBregel

Instagram.com/TheMediocreMama

Ashli Brehm

Facebook.com/BabyOnTheBrehm

Twitter.com/AshliBrehm

Pinterest.com/BabyOnTheBrehm

Sharon Buckley

Facebook.com/FindingVanillaOctopus

Twitter.com/VanillaOctopus

Melissa Charles

Facebook.com/NotAStepfordLifeBlog

Twitter.com/2TheImp

Pinterest.com/NotStepfordLife

Sarah Cottrell

Facebook.com/HousewifePlus

Twitter.com/Housewife_Plus

Pinterest.com/HousewifePlus

Chris Dean

Facebook.com/PixieLifeYourWay

Twitter.com/PixiecdLYW

Pinterest.com/Pixiecd

Instagram.com/Pixiecd

Julia Goddard

This author does not have social media.

Alice Gomstyn

Facebook.com/MildlyInappropriateMommy

Twitter.com/AliceGomstyn

Lea Grover

Facebook.com/pages/Lea-Grover-Author-
Page/162712160438683

Twitter.com/bcmgSuperMommy

Pinterest.com/bcmgSuperMommy

Carrie Groves

Facebook.com/PoniesAndMartinis

Twitter.com/PonyMartini

Pinterest.com/PonyMartini

Instagram.com/TinyTinesTheDog

Amy Hunter

Facebook.com/OutnumberedMother3

Twitter.com/OutNumbMother

Pinterest.com/OutNumbMother

Instagram.com/OutNumberedMother

Susanne Kerns

Facebook.com/TheDustyParachute

Twitter.com/Dusty_Parachute

Pinterest.com/DustyParachute

Instagram.com/TheDustyParachute

Lisa René LeClair

Facebook.com/Sassypiehole

Twitter.com/Sassypiehole

Instagram.com/Sassypiehole

Pinterest.com/Sassypiehole

Kathryn Leehane

Facebook.com/FoxyWinePocket

Twitter.com/FoxyWinePocket

Pinterest.com/FoxyWinePocket

Instagram.com/FoxyWinePocket

Alessandra Macaluso

Facebook.com/PunkWifeCharlotte

Twitter.com/PunkWife

Pinterest.com/AlessandraMac

Instagram.com/missp290

Bethany Meyer

Facebook.com/4GodsSakeBoys

Twitter.com/4GodsSakeBoys

Pinterest.com/4GodsSakeBoys

Amanda Mushro

Facebook.com/QuestionableChoicesInParenting1

Twitter.com/QuestionableCIP

Pinterest.com/AMushro

Instagram.com/QuestionableCIP

Meredith Napalitano

Facebook.com/FromMeredithToMommy

Twitter.com/MeredithToMommy

Pinterest.com/MereToMommy

Instagram.com/MereToMommy

Kate Parlin

Facebook.com/ShakespearesMom

Twitter.com/ShakespearesMom

Pinterest.com/Shakespeare1254

Lucia Paul

Facebook.com/profile.php?id=100009394479324&fref=ts

Twitter.com/DFscrapbook

Cate Pedersen

Facebook.com/CopyCateWritingEditingandCommunications

Twitter.com/CatePedersen

Holly Rust

Facebook.com/MothersGuideToSanity

Twitter.com/HollyRust

Pinterest.com/MG2SANITY

Chris Smyrl

This author does not have social media.

Megan Steusloff

This author does not have social media

Mary Widdicks

Facebook.com/OutmannedMommy

Twitter.com/MaryWiddicks

Pinterest.com/OutmannedMommy

Megan Woolsey

Facebook.com/TheHipMothership

Twitter.com/HipMothership

Pinterest.com/HipMothership6

The Brains
Behind This Book

 ## Natalie Guenther

Natalie, her sweet husband, and their three impressively loud boys spend most of their time at one sporting event or another. She works in the medical field as a social worker. In her spare time she enjoys sitting in silence, eating dinner with other adults and sleeping for more than 5 hours at a time.

 ## Kim Schenkelberg

Kim lost her marbles and married a man who is the youngest of ten. She became a stepmom to his boys who are growing up way too fast. They added two girls and a boy to their clan. She works as an adoption search and reunion specialist by day, a mental health therapist by night and a writer/publisher during her non-existent free time. She laments daily that she is not a trust-fund baby.

Celeste Snodgrass

Celeste, her hilarious husband, two quickly growing kids and two dogs are new transplants to Sioux Falls, SD. She works for an international child welfare and adoption agency. She daydreams of having enough free time to make all the delicious recipes and fun DIY projects she has on her Pinterest boards.

Connect with us!

Facebook.com/ItsReally10Months
Twitter.com/Really10Months
Instagram.com/ItsReally10Months
Pinterest.com/Really10Months
ItsReally10Months.com
ItsReally10Months.com/blog

If you loved this book, you'll love our firstborn!

It's Really 10 Months: Delivering the Truth about the Glow of Pregnancy and Other Blatant Lies
ISBN: 978-0-9888668-1-2
Price: $15.95

Purchase the book at ItsReally10Months.com
Also available on Kindle and other e-reader formats

Use code **A6PSC4M7** for 25% off a copy of *It's Really 10 Months: Delivering the Truth about the Glow of Pregnancy and Other Blatant Lies*